Beyond Public Opinion

Pondering the Public Sphere from a Paris Café

Robert William Deller

Acknowledgments

This book would not have been possible without the encouragement of family members who insisted I find a better way to communicate thoughts than testing their patience to consider them. Additional appreciation is gratefully expressed to Professor W. Scott Haine for his continual advice to remain within the focus on "What would Socrates have said," and of Jürgen Habermas in the latter's context of building communities around the Public Sphere. The book itself would have been impossible without the expert development skills of my wife, Sylvie. Her accommodating patience with my insistence of content focus while she mastered the important elements of format and standardization resulted in this final product.

Preface - Where do we begin?

It is worth asking why more communication is needed to consider the many influential social and political issues surrounding our contemporary lives. The answer seems to fall into two categories. One is that adequate resolution of questions and uncertainties has not yet occurred in spite of reporting in extensive commercial news services and abundant social media. A second is that issues themselves draw less than adequate concern from the public to justify time and thought perceived necessary to address them.

This book takes the position that by focusing discussions on popular issues identified in contemporary media sources, complemented by influential research references, quality of discourse could be heightened. Understanding human value resulting from enhanced discussion is thereby intended. At a minimum, thoughtful consideration of contemporary issues could more readily result.

As a form of discourse, material in this book follows the principle applied in the Agora of Ancient Greece, present in the works of Socrates and Plato. Discourse seeks to expand perspectives, to erase beliefs not satisfying tests of reason. Conversations today around important social issues might reasonably follow what had taken place in eighteenth century England. Where conversations begin doesn't matter because all thought suggests or leads to a single reality - a presence of what Alan White claimed as "coherence in truth."[1]

---

[1] White, Alan, Absolute Knowledge: Hegel and the Problem of Metaphysics, Ohio Univ. Press, 1983.

Issues chosen for this book resulted from randomly selected thoughts shared during conversations over a seven-year period from 2012 to 2018 at one of the many sidewalk cafés in Paris. These conversations were enriched by integrating personal perspectives about social issues with individual understanding from experiences of others. We can know personal truth to the extent we know ourselves, if the Oracle of Delphi has any purpose.[2]

And why not in Paris, capital city sprung with intent to inform through an encyclopedia of contemporary thinking in 1751?[3] While Diderot and his colleagues sought to present contemporary intellectual letters describing what was known or knowable during that period, the idea in more contemporary times is to perpetuate the process of thinking of things rather than representation of things already thought. We find them in public discourse.

Very notably, public discourse as an element of sociability pits its spread in eighteenth century France and other parts of Europe at the time against a backdrop of constraining limitations on breadth of conservative thinking found in Great Britain. One might, as discussed by Ron Vanelli in more contemporary times, consider the expansion of sociability an element of social evolution.[4]

---

[2] Discussed by Robert Graves, in "The Greek Myths: Complete Edition." Penguin, Harmondsworth, 1993. See also, Ionna Konstaninou, "Delphi: the Oracle and its Role in the Political and Social Life of the Ancient Greeks", Hannibal Publishing House, Athens.

[3] See the collaborative translation project for Encyclopedia of Diderot and D'Alembert found at https://quod.lib.umich.edu/d/did/intro.html.

[4] See, Ron Vanelli's "Evolutionary Theory And Human Nature," Open Source CRM Support Forum, found at http://forubbooks.dasoft-hosting.com/?q=Evolutionary+theory+and+human+nature+by+ron+vannelli&ref=http%3A%2F%2Fumdndq3ivk.moe.hm%2F26.html.

Issues ranging from societal concerns to performance of democratic governments appear to occupy the public's constant attention. Although issues represented here originated in a series of personal blogs published during a limited time frame, none was purposefully addressed with a mind toward publication, beyond adding to the *bavardeuse* chatter from several other cafe tables equally engaged with various topics resulting from public concern.

The idea for publication occurred only after a significant number of under-served issues had been identified and discussed. What was determined during that period was that the general public simply does not address important social-political issues with intent to uncover real problems and supporting truths. Mostly, it can be claimed, public conversations amount to each party seeking either to claim validity for a personal view or to impose a personal view on someone else. Nor is there sufficient residual from discussions actually occurring to serve future rumination, intending to "get to the bottom" of those issues influencing public consciousness. It is acknowledged here that material presented in the book may not represent what might be considered deep meaning in contemporary discourse, even though deep meaning is encouraged.

The cafe approach to discussion is not uncommon, considering the perspective offered by Jean-François Lyotard.[5] He considered such conversations attempts to discover meaning against those provided by other chatters who otherwise opt not for full rigor needed for deep understanding. For the latter, issues discussed normally get "tabled" due to lack of patience, expecting others to accept the task of developing meaning. Perhaps benefit from conversations could be sought by revisiting these perspectives, even if

---

[5] See, Jean-François Lyotard. The Differend: Phrases in Dispute. trans. George Van Den Abbeele (Minneapolis, 1988).

only imagined, by transforming misinformed or unsupported perspectives into meaningful content.

We assume, of course, that too many important conversations have not been developed well enough in the mind of the public to pass for truth. Can it be supposed that one person's experience could be supported by explanation, and that such explanation could be shared with another as if with common meaning? How relevant would such phenomenology be for use in social networks in the modern period? Could it have more value or validly for determining meaning than use of the Internet as a medium for blogs? Can individual experiences really be shared across such limited dimensions of expression, much less understood by either party so engaged?

Understanding truth as an objective

At the center of what constitutes truth we find the individual, how each individual perceives and understands self, and how the individual reflects resulting opinions in the social context. Considering government in the Western world and its focus on democracy for supporting society and influencing the way we live, we turn to thinking at the citizen level. It is here we can expect through active participation to assure appropriate governance, at least for a majority. By focusing on the basis for belief, and on different political ideologies, we see how the individual seeks to be governed. At the same time we consider the many issues dealing with how the individual seeks truth to fit in the larger grouping of humanity.

Truth from the individual

Two means are available to learn about ourselves. One is to accept characterization by those around us who observe our behavior and listen to our proclamations. A second is through an internal sense of who we are. Of course, the latter benefits indirectly from relevant value in expressed perspectives of those around us. The intent of this book then is to benefit the individual as a member of a community through discussion in the search for truth, considering input from those around him/her through what occurs in the Public Sphere.6

Believing seems necessary for the human. It becomes essential in the issue of self-awareness, particularly when change is present in the personal environment. Belief seems a means to respond to issues of change through acceptance of new pieces of information as they had already been experienced in history in conjunction with sympathy for one's own acceptance of relevance in change.

We tend to accept as valid those expressions by notable individuals in history which influence our thinking. What did Plato say? What did he mean in saying it? For those more inclined toward religiosity, following the recorded words of Jesus or Mohammed or Confucius is imperative.

Since none of these sources is scientific, could conscious belief based on these sources be developed in a testable manner? Can human belief overcome religious dogma and still be worthy of communicating to others of different rationale? If verbal communication of like belief could occur, would it suggest that rational commonality could result from shared personal experience? Could like belief be better founded through deep thinking?

If nothing were believed, we would have no concern for our environment, our place in it, nor in relationships with other humans. What to believe as truth varies widely depending on sources of influence, independent

---

6 Jûrgen Habermas, "The Structural Transformation of the Public Sphere," Cambridge, trans. 1985.

of how technologically advanced or socially developed individuals are or through the medium by which they communicate.

Thought itself requires some element of belief resulting from either intuition or from reflection. Because thinking appeals to the human mind there is fair expectation that through shared thoughts a single reality could be determined, or approached.

A significant disconnect seems to exist between public perception of political issues and a hidden but influential process taking place around individuals with often untoward results. Citizens appear to react on one hand to societal issues that are real, but hidden, and on the other hand to effects from these issues as they play out. In either case there is inadequate understanding by these citizens for participation in a democratic process requiring a well informed populace, advisedly stated by Thomas Jefferson: "an educated citizenry is a vital requisite for survival of a free people."[7]

The role of the Public Sphere

Arguably, an appropriate venue for citizens to participate in an intelligence seeking process to develop necessary understanding of political issues is the Public Sphere. It is in such setting that issues can be identified with the intent of determining meaning for rules and events influencing daily life. Investigation of meaning behind literal expression of beliefs forms a basis for discussing content and for improved understanding and subsequent citizen action.

---

[7] According to Anna Berkes, as recently as 24 January 2020, this exact quotation has not been found in any of the writings of Thomas Jefferson, although it is accepted as a generally accurate paraphrase of Jefferson's views on education.

A simple process that appears to work, that is, it results in more common-ly shared understanding of the individual's role in events and public issues, begins with identifying an issue of mutual interest. Pieces of the issue are specified, and beliefs concerning each piece of the issue are expressed. Rather than moving toward common acceptance of such beliefs, even if log-ical arrangement of elements is presented, different perspectives for the same elements are elicited. Benefits suit the individual. Together, the ele-ments form a collective frame for considering how the event or public issue can be viewed for benefit within a community of like interests. After itera-tion of each element is enriched by point and counterpoint, thesis and an-tithesis, evaluation, a summary perspective is developed and suggested for contributing to the knowing of self. To the extent wisdom is desired, even if incrementally, this method of evaluation serves the purpose.

Such expansion of discourse suggests what Habermas described in the Public Sphere as "structural transformation."8 Essentially, we propose to influence the individual's sense of participating in society through contribut-ing to public opinion. With this purpose, the notion of a governing State is legitimized through its practice of democracy, at least in contemporary Western societies.

At the same time, we acknowledge that public opinion changes dramati-cally at times to reflect a very fluid base of influencing issues and under-standings. It is with this view in mind that we encourage active debate about issues of public concern and their relevance within a dynamic framework supporting the notion of democracy - after all, a form of government influ-enced by public concern. Purposefully, everyday political talk in non-politi-cal settings, referred to by Graham, Jackson, and Wright as online "third

---

8 Habermas, Op. cit.

spaces,"9 has led to political action favoring enriched thinking from the Public Sphere.

Building community addresses structural transformation in the way it integrates personal perspective with shared understanding with others of like interest. In 2017, Mark Zuckerburg introduced the notion that public networks could provide a means for developing community.10 What resulted was more the effects of group think in which one perspective was shared across a broad spectrum of participation, rather than as a platform for developing thought for appropriate action. While a reasonable gesture by Mr. Zuckerberg, it misses the value brought by individuals who contribute perspectives developed through deep thinking based on difference, sometimes disagreement, rather than from shared opinion expressed by others lacking value from the Public Sphere.

Searching for belief

We might consider differences that separate individual beliefs about a complex universe. Perhaps it is method for determining how to discuss things we hold central to our notion of human existence. No matter what any individual believes, how existence is discussed is central to the one reality we can all share. Each of us seems to seek something, an explanation of what we experience, in order to understand it. If we hold no specific belief in common, understanding whatever it is that binds us is critical to any sin-

---

9 See, Scott Wright, Todd Graham, and Daniel Jackson, "From everyday conversation to political action: Talking austerity in online 'third spaces'", European Journal of Communication, 2015.

10Mark Zuckerberg, "Building Global Community," Facebook, 16 February, 2017.

gle understanding of reality. What anchors this understanding is critical to anything anyone can claim to know.

Perhaps it is method, then, that we hold central to our notion of human existence. No matter what any individual believes, how belief is discussed is central to the one reality we all share. If we hold no belief in common, what it is that binds us is critical to any understanding we develop rationally.

Can we really be held accountable for anything other than participating meaningfully in the search for what cannot be known nor understood? We might disagree on what is and what is not, but the discussion we could have creates merit for whatever it is we accept individually. Perhaps these claims of acceptance could provide a basis for discussing important things, not to cause one to change what is believed but to sharpen the process for determining what is to be believed.

Two people may disagree on the question of whether the current President of the United States should be removed from office prior to the next national election. Each person bases belief on some information, knowledge, or understanding. Even political allegiance requires some measure of belief, even if only emotional. What constitutes this formative process can be discussed without considering the result of the substance itself. Re-evaluation of content could occur as a result of the process of considering.

Specifically, do we base our beliefs on rational elements of truth, or do our beliefs result from dogmatically accepting positions declared by others who lack a basis for rational support in favoring an emotional element far removed from the question addressed? It is the process needed for knowing that provides the value.

On the other hand, two people may agree on whether the President should be removed from office based on different thinking. Each belief might suggest different formative justification. The difference in reasoning provides a valid basis for discussion.

Following Socrates, and a host of other thinkers throughout history supporting need for a rational basis for describing reality, we consider that truth exists when it is demonstrated through cross examination. Awareness of what another person bases rational belief needs not impose change in beliefs. The experience of debate should have influential value for constructing what we believe. Debate provides a way to consider the same information that influences others. It could also show how different belief could result from the same information.

Part I: Ideology - Influences on how to think about what to believe

Dialogue 1. God as an Asymptote

According to Stanley Fish, any claim in literature invites the participation of the reader to develop thought.11 Fish does not advocate subjective interpretation that results in endless competition among interpretations. Rather, he addresses how meaning results from the community operating together.

Virtually everyone at one time or other considers existence of God, or gods, something explaining or justifying existence of humanity, its purpose, its strengths and its frailties. In the United States, differentiation can be found between belief in God as a religious reference to guide one's life or from a scientific perspective of singularity to satisfy rational constructs of existence.

According to a 2017 Pew Research Foundation poll of U.S. adults, eighty percent express some belief in God as described in the Bible.12 Only one in ten, according to the study, does not believe in God of any kind. Almost half of all believers claim to have had some form of communication with their God, whether or not belief is based on religious association.

The result of any deliberation of existence of God as an entity is less the point than consideration of the issue of understanding existence, itself. Is there justification for living? Why does the issue even occur as a question? Is there value in answering it? Or, does the issue exist merely as a matter of

---

[11] See Stanley Fish, "Is There a Text in this Class?", Harvard University Press, 1980.

[12] Pew Research Center, "When Americans Say They Believe in God, What Do They Mean?", found at https://www.pewforum.org/2018/04/25/when-americans-say-they-believe-in-god-what-do-they-mean/

intellectual interest, an abstraction based on signs and symptoms of life, with no requirement for explanation?

Thomas Jefferson and Benjamin Franklin, among early proponents of democratic thought in the United States, provided explanations addressing a single entity from which collective human existence could be explained.13 Franklin, in a perspective reflecting interest but not concern, claimed, "I do not dogmatize upon, having never studied it, and think it is needless to busy myself with it now."14

We may be challenged to seek meaning for what we think exists. Our beliefs are expected to survive tests of either experience or rationality. No belief escapes such test, even for devout individuals who claim willingness to accept what is claimed without question as a matter of faith in the individual's existence. Acceptance of any belief from faith relies on an authority claimed as a divine source, a priori. Even for such individual acceptance, some form of verification occurs, and it is applied incrementally to be increasingly convincing, logically or spiritually.

For any thinking individual, the distance between what can be explained rationally (scientifically) and what constitutes reality by imagination, or by claimed spiritual experience characterized through the mind of the human being, approaches zero as personal belief and scientifically supported reality converge.

The notion of democracy behaves similarly. As an ideal it is open to interpretation by those who discuss it. Actualization depends on how it is ex-

---

13 See John Fea, Religion And Early Politics: Benjamin Franklin and His Religious Beliefs." Pennsylvania Heritage Magazine, Volume XXXVII, Number 4 - Fall 2011.

14 Benjamin Franklin letter to Ezra Stiles, 9 March 1790, Benjamin Franklin Autobiography, Oxford World Classics, 1998.

perienced. Basis for belief ranges from rationalized ideal to personal experience.

The Asymptote

Many will object to reference of God in mathematical terms, but the relationship could be more appropriate than such objection would allow.

In a rational sense, the asymptote of converging realities follows a mathematical equation, generally in the form, $y = f(x)$. That is, following an equation for a straight line, positions of a dependent variable approach positions of an independent variable as their respective values converge - theoretically when the unexplained difference reaches the value of zero. In other words, the value for difference between the dependent and independent variables becomes zero as the measures of the two come closer together. They don't actually ever resolve the linear point of tangency because there always remains in the function of the relationship something which is unexplained, sort of an obstruction to knowledge due to what is unknown, or unknowable.

Other equations for straight lines exist, but the hyperbola is convenient to show a transitive relationship with limits between an ideal and a behavior.

We can accumulate increasing amounts of explanation for what constitutes reality, but we haven't been able to explain all of the difference. Probably, we never will. What we can't explain we relegate to a knowledge held only by a supernatural entity. Or, we vacate the issue of knowing everything by claiming through religious thought that the whole notion of knowing has no meaningful value for the human. Alternatively, we can tolerate the unknown segment of reality by gradually reducing it through rational thought or scientific evidence, that is, reducing what we don't know about it.

More to the point, asymptotes are found in more relationships than in geometric forms. Unexplainable things seem always as impediments to attaining the goal of understanding them entirely.

Is the view of democracy as an ideal any different?

Notion of Sovereignty

At some distance from what most people accept as contrast between what is knowable and what is not, we again find the often heated debate regarding existence of a sovereign God. We don't seem to get much further into explanation because only a relatively few people are willing to investigate the phenomenon of what seems not knowable. Too easily the debate is dismissed by various incomplete notions regarding what is or is not knowable, or what is or is not God. Or, why does God exist as sovereign such that understanding is not necessary or even appropriate?

How far into any discussion are we willing to venture, and at the same time retain sufficient patience to apply what is discovered through discussion, to how we accept the unexplained portion of reality? We live and we die. In the meantime why not just accept that there is sovereignty in God (or no such sovereignty at all) and let it go at that?

Of course, what is thought to be known, or thought not to be knowable, is unique to the individual. That means essentially that each person's perception of what constitutes God is unique (varying from zero to infinity on a scale of sovereign powers associated with God). Nothing wrong with that, if we could stop there.

The uncertainty with which we claim existence of sovereignty under God causes us doubt. (Who could not doubt what is not known?) Seeking common acceptance of what is thought to be known or thought to be unknown becomes a basic tenet of religious belief, a catechism. What to believe is a matter for a constitution for society to accept as formal guidance to control social behavior, or as behavior of government to assure support to or control of the society. What it assures for the sake of society and how it is to be recognized can be expected literately from its words. Less certain is what we might share in common about the meaning of these same words.

Dispute can be anticipated from those who claim no doubt in what they believe. For them, it is impossible to reach a common level on what might be a continuum of the knowable or rational. What is thought by these individuals to be known is held in common only as others claim the same basis of acceptance.

As a form of dogma it represents a constitutional explanation of what is real about an issue, representing a common point as they reach agreement in their respective appreciation for what is known. A set of behavioral rules and basic beliefs supports such dogma. This dogma substitutes for the asymptote without allowing movement toward getting closer to what could be known or understood, but it provides the stability of supporting a status quo. It limits knowledge from being extended into the space of the unknown and thus limits downside of uncertainty.

We've all heard, or participated in, discussions pitting God (the intelligent designer) against science (the explainer). Few people accept that a real and necessary relationship exists between the two, even if only asymptotically. Rather, an argument results in how science has been wrong in explaining reality based on faith and how religion has not been able to explain phenomena of existence in a more concrete manner than to categorically assign it with all its unknown character to the realm of acceptance.

Could a religion emerge based on acceptance of what is not known that includes a system of continual investigation and restatement of what is known, leaving space for the asymptote of the unexplained?

Arguments

Investigation is needed to address arguments resulting from believing what democratic government may or may not do. While not characteristic of all global societies, those in northern and western hemispheres tend to consider relevance of belief in God as a benevolent influence on how their respective countries should be governed. One might wonder, at least rationally, if democracy is in any way related to religion. Both seem to rest on an undeveloped logic providing support. Both exist through a basis of need for trust in managing the human condition of incompleteness.

One can note religious symbols present in democratic culture in the United States, to consider one example of a country whose government seems devoted to protective care provided by a supernatural existence while rejecting dependence on religious belief as a constitutional priority. In spite of language in the United States Constitution assuring that government would not unduly prefer one religion over another or preferring non-religion over religion of any kind, political leaders such as George Washington supported the practice of religious belief in considering appropriate government rules and behavior.15

---

[15] John C. Fitzpatrick, "The writings of George Washington from the original manuscript sources, 1745-1799. United States George Washington Bicentennial Commission and published by authority of Congress, 1931. Throughout his life, Washington often spoke of "Providence" as a source of benign protection for the American colonists.

The phrase, "In God We Trust," is prominent on American currency, as well as inclusion of the phrase, "One nation under God," in the Pledge of Allegiance to the American Flag.16 American currency contains the language, "Annuit Coeptis" (providence has favored our undertakings) above the square pyramid on the reverse side of the American one-dollar note. The currency in Great Britain contains a similar appeal for providence on its bank notes. By careful inspection of the specie, and a measure of imagination, one can notice other symbols, such as pagan and satanic stars as well as the Star of David.

In contradiction to popular religious beliefs claimed to have been handed down from immigrant practices, resistance is cited as evident on the American dollar and British pound suggesting influence from an Illuminati, an elite group associated with ideals of secular world control. This is especially evident in the wording, "NOVUS ORDO SECLORUM," appearing under the seal on the American dollar and meaning new secular order and implying sovereignty over religious influence.17 Even in France, while claiming complete secular focus, the role of the Church through social influence is evident.18

As a final comment on the issue of sovereignty under God, consider the phrase in the oath of office expected of a president or other high ranking of-

---

16 See, Public Law, 83-396, 68 Stat. 249, H.J.Res. 243. enacted June 14, 1954.
The phrase, "one Nation under God" was added during the Administration of Dwight Eisenhower in responding to the growing "God-less" Communist influence.

17 Explanation found at, https://greatseal.com/mottoes/seclorum.html

18 For discussion of secular and religious freedom in democracy practiced in France, found at https://www.diplomatie.gouv.fr/en/coming-to-france/france-facts/secularism-and-religious-freedom-in-france/article/secularism-and-religious-freedom-in-france.

ficial being sworn into service to the U.S. government. "So help me God" brings clearly in alignment the relationship between government and religion,19 in spite of the Enterprise Clause appearing in the First Amendment to the U.S. Constitution.20 In responding to this oath of office, does the president ask for supplication, thus implicitly diminishing power for the leader who must seek and accept help or guidance from a more sovereign entity? Consider President George W. Bush's claim that he was on a mission from God to lead the U.S. against tyranny in Iraq in 2003.21

As democracy defines the structure of most countries in what is considered the developed world, one must focus specifically on the belief issues of the public, to the extent there is participation from this sector in the formation and process of democracy.

The reality for democracy is that it exists as an ideal, something strived for as an endpoint to reflect a government developed to support expectations of its citizens. These expectations of democracy thereby reflect beliefs and behaviors of citizens. When the State attempts to influence these beliefs and behaviors, other than through constitutional language, distortion in the meaning of democracy exists. One might claim that democracy can seek its own end when it is free to evolve consistent with the process designed by its constitution to reflect interests and values of citizens, as an asymptote.

---

[19] The phrase, "so help me God," has been part of the official oath of office for non-presidential offices since 1862. The founders decided to require an oath for federal and state officials — absent a religious test. Reference found at, https://history.house.gov/Institution/Origins-Development/Oath-of-Office/

[20] "Congress shall make no law respecting an establishment of religion, or prohibiting the free exercise thereof..."

[21] Paul Harris, "Bush says God chose him to lead his nation," The Guardian, 3 Nov. 2003.

A simple truth

Of course, God is not an asymptote. Concept of God can be approached, much as anything definable can be aligned with another when their perceivable dimensions are matched one to one. God is not so rationally characterized. The brain does not provide a necessary path for understanding God. The brain does not comprehend lack of dimension, absence of systems to measure existence. To understand God, we depend on shared experiences resulting from awareness of our own existence.

Very often we take the opportunity to anticipate life's primary causes, and similarly what happens after we no longer exist - at least in the form we find ourselves in this life. We seek understanding but come up empty when addressing these issues rationally with an idea that some meaning really exists to justify living. We don't know more than that we just don't know. Nevertheless, much of our time is spent in contemplating the questions - is there God? Does a God need to be?

Those who believe the questions have no merit, or no relevance in their lives, must still search to find succor with others who share the same acceptance of the human as static in a fixed existence literally based on printed gospel.

Seekers of explanation however pose these questions among themselves expecting to find answers or segments of answers to allow stitching together full meaning. The best these individuals can do is to approach a position that is rationally, or even scientifically, supported. It's the best that can be expected.

As humans we all seem in need of explanation - what is or what explains. Reality seems beyond our ability to trust in a means to understand it without bringing it into the Public Sphere. That is where answers can be posed and examined based on rationality or on non-rational personal values. Whether we accept an answer through unquestioned faith or through reason, resolution requires some form of interactive communication of what may be understood, or even shared.

A God that exists can be found in the asymptote, the difference between what is and what we believe it to be. If existence of God is acceptably real, from what evidence can such God be characterized? Why would it have the limiting characteristics of a humanoid if claims are made that all the world is created in His image?

The humanoid is itself a changed phenomenon following existence of all life's evolution from the first instance. Since there is no measurable space in the asymptote one would expect to be able to characterize a God found in this space to manifest whatever the imagination - educated, result of extrasensory intervention, or something else, or whatever results comes from a rational construct for understanding, or even just unsupported acceptance. Such element of identity reflects perspective of the individual, unique as he/she is in the universe. No further definition for God is appropriately meaningful to the "true believer," other than through myth or poetry.

Dialogue 2. An objective for social contract

According to the Stanford Encyclopedia of Philosophy, a social contract forms a mutually dependent relationship between citizens and the governing democracy that supports them.22 Originating in the earlier time of Epicurus, it now takes its modern form following expressions of Thomas Hobbes in the post Enlightenment period and more recently, of John Locke and Jean-Jacques Rousseau. The idea to "collectively enforce social arrangements" reflects the objective under which a representative government operates to serve the usually dependent communities: society and government.

In an attempt to assure moral consensus in the face of religious diversity found in society at the time, Hugo Grotius introduced the idea that natural rights based on scientific evidence rather than on religious sentiment enabled self-preservation of the individual.23 Thomas Hobbes is credited with explaining the importance of such arrangements - why they both must exist.24 Hobbes presupposed theoretical societies, those characterizing government found in the first writings anchoring support for democracy. At the foundation of this theory in practice is a constitution developed for each State representing how a government - its duties and its limitations, is to be formed on behalf of society. While Hobbes supported authoritarian govern-

---

22 Found at, https://plato.stanford.edu/entries/contractarianism-contemporary/

23 John Dunn and Ian Harris, (eds.) *Grotius*, vols. 1–2 (Cheltenham, UK: Edward Elgar Publishing), 1997.

24 See Gough, J. W. *The Social Contract* (Oxford: Clarendon Press, 1936), pp. 2–3, for discussion of social contract as viewed by Thomas Hobbes.

ment, more liberal thinkers followed with a social contract arrangement that aligned more favorably with liberal aspects of man's freedom in nature.

Essentially, by the end of the eighteenth century, a social contract proscribed in general terms or conditions how society was to be governed. It aligned with how members of the society might benefit from inalienable liberties found as rights in nature. Citizens promised obedience to rulers in exchange for promised protection and good governance. To the extent society is expected to keep its part of the bargain, government leaders must keep theirs. Or so it was understood implicitly.

What seems to differ among social contracts is method by which government leadership is determined. Hobbes claimed that while citizens required total government control, later more liberal thinkers allowed that if leaders misgovern, as reflected by expressions of citizen dissatisfaction, the social contract would be broken with allegiance coming to an end. Seemingly under the latter arrangement, society had the upper hand.

John Locke claimed citizens incapable of objectively selecting such leadership, due in his own thinking to lack of training among citizens and resultant unawareness of requirements for leadership.25 On the other hand, Jean-Jacque Rousseau believed that self-rule in democracy to be the best way to ensure welfare and to maintain individual freedoms under rules following natural law.26 The United States Declaration of Independence reflects this more liberally based Lockean concept.27

---

[25] Locke, John. Second Treatise on Government, 1689.

[26] Jean-Jacque Rousseau believed in self-rule as a basis for democracy. See, Leo Strauss. "On the Intention of Rousseau." Social Research 14 (1947): pp. 455-487.

[27] A Century of Lawmaking for a New Nation. U.S. Congressional Documents and Debates, 1774 - 1875. Journals of the Continental Congress, Volume 5, Page 510 of 856.

Social contract theories evolved in the 19th century from several theoretical directions. Jeremy Bentham's utilitarianism (for the sake of the whole), Hegelianism (for the sake of self), and Marxism (for the sake of classless society), were later revised in the 20th century, notably in the form of a "what if" experiment by John Rawls (Veil of Ignorance),28 and under a backdrop of liberal progressive development incorporating ideas that refine the nature of free thought. The contemporary notion presented by Robert Nozick, claims that wealth can be retained as a means to secure the individual's welfare in a rapidly changing world.29 Nozick suggested that respect for human rights covered areas of life, liberty, property and contract apart from arbitrary determination found in nature of how justice was to be determined. This is in opposition from Rousseau's earlier claim that owning anything in nature was against principles of freedom.30 Indeed, in conflict with classical liberal principles what was prominent in influences from the Framers of the U.S. Constitution was indeed ownership of property, including slaves.

The Objective for Social Contract

Social contracts are relationships we find in society in which individuals relinquish some elements claimed for liberty with an assurance from government that services for other freedoms will be provided. To Hobbes, humans have so many self-destructive foibles that governmental protection

28 For a discussion of John Rawls's Theory of Justice, found at http://www.hup.harvard.edu/catalog.php?isbn=9780674000780&content=reviews

29 Robert Nozick, Anarchy, State, and Utopia. Contributors: Basic Books. New York, 1974.

30 See discussed in James Koppenberg, "*Trial and Error*," Toward Democracy, Oxford University Press, New York, 2016.

against citizens, among other services, is necessary to maintain order in society, assuming humans are justified in finding it of interest to not live alone.31 Personal independence or self-reliance never had a chance, even with government as a protective surrogate. Consequently, it wasn't appropriate to believe that individuals were entitled to liberty, unless uncontrolled self-destruction of the species was the order of the day. So Hobbes would claim. By the time Rousseau came on the scene, responsibility for personal safety and security was less dependent on a governing body than on relationships developed among peers.

That leaves a question normally taken up by politically minded anthropologists: Does humanity exist as a collection of unique individuals, each responsible to him/herself for behavior primarily and then to others secondarily, by benefiting from the opportunity of self actualization? Or, do individuals live in communities that support sharing and mutual dependency?

Under American exceptionalism, are individuals discrete elements in a big picture? Do individuals each constitute complete self-reliant entities? Is the individualism championed by American democracy appropriate to who we are as a species, while conflicting with obligations of mutual dependence in society?

Consider that although all individuals come into existence the same way, each is measurably different. They vary physically (size, weight, gender). They have different motivations (likes and dislikes). Their influences differ (wants and needs), as well as how they influence each other through interpersonal relationships.

---

31 See a discussion of Hobbes and use of scientific thinking to support the claim for government in G. Herbert, *Thomas Hobbes: The Unity of Scientific and Moral Wisdom*. Vancouver: University of British Columbia Press, 1989.

But, individuals are not isolated single entities. They need and depend on each other. They benefit from community. They contribute to community. They are elements in perpetuating family lines. They might even be members of communities of like thought or behavioral patterns influenced by other than DNA structures, at least to the extent such structures are known.

And, individuals don't endure forever, at least not in the limited state between birth and death we seem to understand them. They also seem limited by an unwillingness, other than through a religious perspective, to consider any alternative to an end of life. It is accepted, however, that all are born and all will die. We only speculate as individuals about before-life and after-life periods, being left to wonder about such things as if each of us exists as a discrete character in a drama of continuing life.

Coming into being is a process, one we associate with the passing of time. We age, we mature, then we are no more, not as we knew of ourselves during the process. What causes each individual to be different at the end from what they were at the beginning? Were they inherently complete as universals as Aristotle would have argued, or following a predesigned nature after Plato's eidos? Or does the individual gain or lose character elements during the process of being?

How does community relate to individuality? Why is it that individuals do, after all, depend on others? Perhaps they are responsible not for their own success as living entities, but for the success of societies in which they find themselves. Could it be that society itself is the life force that survives? If all that humans are capable of while they live is to die as they were born without having developed individually or as members of a matured society, then otherwise, all might seem wasted energy.

So, what is it that endures: self or society? Is the imperfection individuals find in themselves, as emphasized by religion, due to a need to build a different more inclusive form of life for the sake of a more whole community, or from a different perspective for "exceptional" self?

And what of Rousseau's concept of contract with the State? He could have, even if implicitly, characterized a value for living in a more inter-dependent manner as community and not as individuals. The living wouldn't be as an individual who passes into an after-life. It would be the whole of society, or segment of society, that survives, completed by a generational evolution of perfecting a relationship between its integrated social elements as a more inclusive species.

We are instructed by quantum physics that more than three physical dimensions exist in space. The human perception is limited to only three. If this quantum physics claim is correct, there is more than only a three-dimensional individual to the whole of life. What could influence the sense of existence by awareness of additional dimensions? Should social contract consider and accommodate such existence?

Social contract as valid for democracy

It is easy to claim that democracy is in practice all it was meant to be, even as a living form. Just as easily, democracy could be claimed to be different as practiced among each of the many forms of government enlisting it. But no matter how it is claimed, or even practiced, the focus is on citizen welfare as based on freedoms specifically for the individual as found in nature, and not on community.

At the same time, society benefits from democratic government: for services and for control applicable to groups. As has been observed in virtually every society, individuals reflect attitudes and beliefs existing in mutual support or on conflicts demonstrated through groups. The logic involved in resolving conflicts between groups was advanced by Hobbes in Leviathan with a scientific demonstration that government was required to settle disputes between groups and to avoid civil war developed by groups.32

Government on the other hand, reacting to concerns for avoiding chaos in society, can easily develop into despotism, or in oppressive absolute power, when its authority extends beyond that needed to resolve conflict. Even Machiavelli in the sixteenth century warned against unnecessary applications of State power believed to stabilize government leadership but resulting in citizen discontent and rebellion against authority.33

In contemporary time, democracy representing a concomitant relationship between state and citizens is acknowledged almost without question. While citizen power is systematically limited directly to voting and indirectly to various forms of representation, power of the State is virtually unlimited - to the extent it is enforceable without extra-legal resistance from citizens. Potentially, the social contract supposedly protecting citizens against excessive applications of power becomes malleable as government applies more or less questionable justification for any growth in its base of authority.

A simple truth

Basing government on what seems a foundation of morality presumed from elements found in nature denies a more fundamental truth of citizens behaving according to the same laws of nature. We arrive at this disconnect

---

32 Ibid.

33 Niccolò Machiavelli (1961), The Prince, London: Penguin, ISBN 978-0-14-044915-0.

when elite groups of citizens claim forms of superiority based on natural selection or on degrees of entitlement earned, naturally.

To build contract around natural law requires acceptance of all manner of human behavior, one element of which could without care be destructive relative to behaviors associated with humanity as a collective whole, as societies. One can have good intention toward supporting self but detrimental to benefits for others, all within the framework of individual rights from nature.

If inherent human differences are not understood as unique to the individual, means to support them cannot be found. Listening to difference without imposing personal bias requires an active desire to understand the larger element of nature and how the human experience exists within it. If citizens have responsibility within the Social Contract, discussions of difference among individuals must occur to find elements of common value for the purpose of building democracy.

Issues surrounding social contract are vague, as finding meaning depends largely on interpretation of individual claims and opinions. Yet, value of democracy for all society is based on these meanings. We turn to discussion to both express opinion and belief and to evaluate those of others. Seeking meaning is the objective of the Public Sphere, and forthright expression of position is imperative for finding commonality and support for government leaders elected to represent public values. A method for understanding difference is needed so that difference can be seen as a value rather than something to negate through majority rule.

A citizenship willing to benefit from democratic governance without at least monitoring and mindful of services and controls legislated must we willing to accept whatever level of authoritarian control translates to power for leaders rather than consistent with tenets of a social contract instituted by and for them.

Dialogue 3. Social stability: peace or the economy

John Maynard Keynes argued in 1920 following World War I and the Versailles Treaty that an economic stability was imperative for a much more generous peace.34 He passed over issues of justice and fairness in arriving at this response to the crisis at the time. Determining peace on a rational basis rather than on sentiment resulting from elements found in peacetime deserves consideration.

An interesting perspective on peace and the economy is gained by considering peace as a monetary unit. Imagine states bartering among themselves on the basis of how much peace could be exchanged or supported in order to attain political and economic stability.

Defining peace is naturally required. If one claims existence of complete stressless freedom from disturbance, or disposition of tranquillity, a period in which there is no militancy, how might we think about war as an opposite of peace?

Von Clausewitz famously claimed war as a violent response from failed politics, "the continuation of politics by other means," he claimed.35 Against this still popular view can be seen that war fundamentally exists as a fundamental element of human behavior, unresolved conflict existing between different perspectives and beliefs of individuals, or of whole societies

---

34 See John Maynard Keynes, The Economic Consequences of the Peace, Harcourt, Brace and Howe, New York, 1920.

35 Carl von Clausewitz, On War. Howard and Paret, eds, Princeton University Press, 1989.

by extension. This contradiction to Clausewitz's perspective is provided by Michel Foucault who claimed that politics or policy follows the need to address war, a condition existing as a fundamental human element in society.36

Could units of peace be exchanged for units of economic wealth as inspired by Bretton Woods? The focus for the post World War II Bretton Woods agreement was through an obligation for each country to adopt a policy to maintain trade based on a monetary unit of measure that could be converted based on a given standard.37 The purpose addressed a heretofore lack of cooperation among non-participating countries and to prevent devaluation of the various currencies conforming to a standard. Units of interstate trade could be transformed to degrees of peace. Imagine one State demanding access to mineral deposits of another country in exchange for military support to ward off aggressive neighboring States seeking expansion. More often, political favors are requested from one State to benefit another in exchange for military support.38

If peace were to be considered a bargaining unit, that is, one state trades conditions of non-militant behavior to accommodate conditions of wealth, would assurance that elimination of military conflict follows? Could maintaining peace be regarded as an obligation? Does threat of non-compliance or non-cooperation, or negative-peace, produce the same discontinuity as existed for different monetary units before the Bretton Woods agreement?

---

36 Michel Foucault, Society Must be Defended, F. Ewald, ed. Lectures at the College of France, Macmillan, 2003.

37 Found at, https://www.thebalance.com/bretton-woods-system-and-1944-agreement-3306133.

38 Discussed at, https://www.imf.org/external/about/histend.htm

Bretton Woods set a standard for controlling convertible monetary values, basing it on a fixed value for a specified unit of gold. For a significant period of time the agreement was successful in supporting international trade. But not forever. The linkage between monetary units and gold bullion was broken in 1971 when then U.S. President Richard Nixon suspended the dollar's convertibility to gold. The resulting arrangement for stabilizing trade was based on the U.S. dollar, and world economy went through reactive adjustment.

At that time, development of new weapons destabilized conditions of peace. Desire for peace required feeding the military industrial complex in demonstrating that peace could be exchanged for economic growth.

Actions redefining the basis for currency exchange create difficulty with planning a future from theoretical models of supply and demand. Such difficulty resulting from a flexible Bretton Woods standard based on market dynamics could be seen in variable applications of peace to influence economic conditions.

A not often discussed but necessary difference between theory and practice is observed in dealing with peace as a commodity. Consider the Joint Comprehensive Plan of Action related to Iran's potential threat of developing nuclear weapons in which economic sanctions were put in place to assure peace.39

Early Greek philosophers, notably Plato, developed a reasonable approach to understanding nature, matching theory and practice. Unique models for all things existed, or pre-existed for Plato, for addressing behavior of all humanity. It remains only to discuss models in order to understand rela-

---

39 See Arms Control Association, The Joint Comprehensive Plan of Action (JCPOA) at a Glance, found at https://www.armscontrol.org/factsheets/JCPOA-at-a-glance

tionships in a way that could predict future behavior. Plato's concern was most clearly illustrated in the Meno dialogue. Here he demonstrated through verbal interaction how an uneducated house boy understands geometric principles, and could extrapolate from them.40

Martin Jay asks, "How can we know what is claimed in the absence of experience?"41 This support for value of experience to legitimize theory is known today as Plato's Problem. The theory that peace results from lack of military engagement would not survive in considering peace as a condition other than threat of physical aggression.

How might peace in any condition other than physical aggression be determined without understanding or experiencing a different notion of peace? Conditions of peace may not exist just because of cessation of militancy, at least according to Foucault. What past experience of cessation of militancy is there to consider? Neither World War I nor World War II created conditions of peace since internal conflicts continued subsequent or even consequent to both examples.

Einstein provided an approach to the issue through mathematics. In his "Geometry and Experience" Einstein stated, "How is it that mathematics, being after all a product of human thought, is so admirably appropriate to the objects of reality?"42 With rational human reason then, could peace be experienced merely by using thought to fathom the properties of peace as a

------

40 Jacob Klein, *A Commentary on Plato's* Meno. Chapel Hill: University of North Carolina Press, 1965.

41 Martin Jay, Songs of Experience, Modern American and European Variations on a Universal Theme, University of California Press, January 2005.

42 Discussed in E. P. Wigner, "The unreasonable effectiveness of mathematics in the natural sciences, Communications on Pure and Applied Mathematics. **13**: 1–14. 1960.

real thing? Thought produces axioms as "implicit definitions" to be verified by experience. Peace is a product of experience.

John Dewey claimed the Greeks were wrong to debate pure reason as form for intelligence gathering rather than learning through experience, as if experience were in opposition to what is either theoretically eternal or unbridgeable. The Greek's fetish of developing universal truth or relationships disregarded the value of practical activity in the world. Is peace to be understood then through experience or through theory?43

Another perception of difficulty in associating reason with experience was provided by Immanuel Kant who claimed in a 1795 essay that perpetual peace is practically unachievable, whether or not experience demonstrates it.44 Could there be a more fundamental peace than that which results from cessation of military aggression? Would such peace result from barter for economic advantage without threat of military action?

An example from the Middle East

Nuclear power is not the primary issue underpinning conflict between Iran and the United States with its international allies, at least rationally. For reasons most would accept, neither side possesses self-serving interest in exercising a nuclear war. Actually, one could follow several different paths of rationality to explain current conflict between the several sovereign States interacting with Iran.

---

43 For Dewey's discussion of the classical notion of experience, see especially his Reconstruction in Philosophy, chapter 4, New York, 1920.

44 Immanuel Kant, To perpetual peace: a philosophical sketch, Hackett Publishing, 2003.

The United States wants, among its other motives, to assure its access to Middle East petroleum, even if a smaller percent comes from that region than from its own repositories or from neighbor countries in the Western Hemisphere (Canada or Mexico). It offers peace from military action for economic values envisioned through cooperation.

Bilateral accommodation is shared between the U.S. and Israel (for more than one reason). This accommodation is supported by a strong Israel capable of defending itself against its aggressive neighbors (either resulting from U.S. strengthening Israel, or from weakening Israel's enemies).

Many countries in the Middle East represent threats related to both items above, but Iran has been the most intransigent (originating from U.S. commitment to the Shah against Ruhollah Khomeini, a Shiite cleric, but exacerbated by President Trump's withdrawal from the Joint Comprehensive Plan of Action). Saudi Arabia is the only Arab country in the region with which the United States has had a dependable and peaceful relationship: trade of access for protection. (Saudi Arabia has its own enemies among the Arab states in the Middle East.)

The United States economy depends on development, shipping, markets and currency supply. With stability in the Middle East, the United States could resolve all these dependencies. Since most if not all economic models are based on borrowing from the future and paying back with future earnings, this means markets cannot remain constant. They must be expanding and demanding. Peace as a commodity would follow; demand for peace influences economic need.

Military engagement is one element which can create expanding markets. Demands for services during and after military engagement are virtually endless. New markets resulting from war are elements supporting economic growth through periods of peace.

The economic infrastructure of the United States is designed, operates, and now depends on both elements in the item above: military action and military supply. Any new requirement, or even potential for growth, would cause a need to "retool" the economic infrastructure. There is limited capital available to do this. (China as a source of capital seems unwilling at this moment to continue investing in the questionable economy of the United States, or interest in weakening its own economic expansion by having to compete against a strengthened United States position. Japan at the moment lacks available capital.) So, promoting military and commercial market expansion is key to economic stability for the United States in the future, claiming assurance of peace.

In order for new markets to emerge, there must be adequate levels of spending existing within the markets, and there must be continuing demand for United States output. Both of these elements are suffering at the moment. Military expansion remains the greatest potential for economic viability. That requires combat and selling equipment into a market engaged in military activity (for example, through perpetuating NATO's dependency on the U.S. for its expanding military role).

Existing at the same time is a moral imperative claiming that Western nations of the world, led by the United States since World War I, must come to the aid of other countries in need, no matter how this need arises. President Wilson during World War I and President Roosevelt during World War II were successful (by different methods) in rallying American citizens to support war. In each case, justification from the perspective of government was economic expansion, beyond simply economic stability.

The media has been supportive ever since. Media is underpinned by corporate self-empowerment. The extent of reach for corporate power is seen in Citizens United v. Federal Elections Commission (2010) and in a mostly sympathetic Supreme Court. Corporate power now has such a strong political influence on government that its economic model and dependencies on growth dictate how the government moves and even what citizens believe about need for growth.

Iran has all the potential needed to satisfy demands for supporting a military infrastructure (in spite of the general warning against support to a military-industrial complex from former President Eisenhower).45 International military activity in Iraq has all but ended, and only a U.S. corporate infrastructure remains. Afghanistan fighting is diminishing for the moment and local resistance to any Western presence in that country is increasing.

A "controlled Iran" would have the capacity for stabilizing U.S. access to Middle East petroleum, reducing tension from Islamic claimants, easing conflicts between Israel and its Arab neighbors, and providing markets for military expression and supply. The media is poised to contribute to a supporting rationale, and United States political leaders dependent on "corporate obligations" demonstrate how the American population can be led to believe anything they are told, so long as the language contains nationalistic citizenship requirements, favorable economic indicators, and honorable need for self satisfaction.46 Eclectic borrowing from history provides adequate

---

45 Discussed at, https://www.history.com/this-day-in-history/eisenhower-warns-of-military-industrial-complex.

46 Discussed by Yi Shin Tang in "*Complicity and Omissions*," The International Trade Policy for Technology Transfers, Kluwer Law International, 2009.

rationale for media to support anything from prisoner treatment to religious captivation. The notion of internal peace prevails.

In balance, by perpetuating claims against nuclear expansion, a certain drama exists that perpetuates a need to build military presence from the West (not only the United States) while at the same time justifying support to Israel and Saudi Arabia in exchange for their cooperation in the name of peaceful stability in the Middle East.

As long as Iran's influence can be marginalized by sanctions or by threat (two United States nuclear-based carriers in the Persian Gulf, for example), a status quo is maintained in which the military industrial complex can remain healthy. Corporate America can be satisfied, and political leaders in the West (mostly United States and Europe at the moment) can continue policies promoting support to growth of their respective industrial capacities, while their rhetoric directs attention of citizens to believe in the inevitability or threat of nuclear war.

Is peace not therefor considered a commodity?

A simple truth

Peace should not depend on definitional issues, as might be appropriate for economic messaging. Peace is a condition reflecting stable balance of personal values. It favors not the individual but the result of all individuals living together. To the extent the economy could reflect the totality of all its definable issues, peace and the economy could be exchanged for one another. What is key is need to demonstrate how balance for each of the two comparatives could be discussed to find a single element in common. How, indeed, can a rationally based issue be compared with an issue lacking acceptance of how it could be measured?

Expression of citizen values is key to understanding how policy should be balanced between economic need and imperative for peace. If left to political determination these values would too easily run afoul of public interest. Therefore, public discussions of merit for alternative political positions are imperative.

Influence from the Public Sphere can be instrumental in influencing policy makers. Are conditions of peace more in demand by the public than economic growth? Who should make this determination in a democracy if not "a well informed populace"?

Another way to view the tradeoff between peace and economy is to measure one against the other. Which is more important for the individual's survival? Which is more important for survival of the State?

Dialogue 4. Freedom for the Individual

Among the many bantered terms in the English language freedom stands out as one of the most frequently pronounced while among the many misunderstood.

Uncertainty in understanding freedom occurs early in the fabled Pericles speech reported by Thucydides in ancient Greece in which citizens were tasked for access to freedom to relinquish their lives for the State.47 Relinquish their lives for the State? In contrast, Plato later asserted that every member of Greek society should be free to express himself and to basically contemplate his own destiny in support of society.48 The subjectivity in who constitutes the member class or the member's perspective for freedom creates additional vagueness.

A present interpretation drawn from documents characterizing American democracy shows freedom more as a personal view than might be considered reasonable for society taken as a whole.49 Again, we are left with lack of comprehension for personal views on freedom.

---

47 History of the Peloponnesian War, trans, William Smith, Jones & Co. London, 1881.

48 Lutz, Ralph H, The History of the Concept of Freedom, Bulletin of the American Association of University Professors, Vol. 36, No. 1, pp. 18-32.

49 Tocqueville, Alexis de (1988). *Democracy in America*. Edited by J. P. Mayer. New York: Harper Perennial, pp. 659-660.

The view of Self

We can speak of living as a physiological behavior in which the life form uses energy from the environment to sustain itself. But, the process is not eternal, as the individual eventually succumbs to the inadequacies of the environment, and his/her own fallibility, to sustain one's existence. Thus, the human species finds the period of living as having a beginning and an ending.

A meta-level of existence is occasionally discussed in which the human form is overlaid by other influential forms, more sophisticated or more advanced, arrived at through a process of maturation over time. It is seen as an element of evolution. Could it be claimed that the self in one generation is a higher form than a self in previous generations. Are we members of a higher life form than the lives of Thucydides or Plato?

The life of the human species, following the evolutionary pattern of all other species, contains an element of existence apart from only the physical. Following the ideas of John Dewey, we see in any living human a personal nature found above or other than the physical.50 Thus, the individual is more than physical, an element enlarged by its personal experience within its environment. It learns as it advances during an aging process insofar as it takes advantage of an increased capacity to understand its environment and itself within this environment.

Due to inability to understand all aspects of the self and its environment, the individual develops a means to cope against a wall of ignorance. This coping is a manufacturing of concepts that "forgive" the individual for its

---

50 Abdul Muhit, Notions of 'Experience' in John Dewey's Philosophy, Philosophy and Progress, Vols. LIII-LIV, January-June, July-December, 2013.

inability to understand all things. Or the self is castigated for lack of success within the environment. Thus, the human's ability to understand is limited to the extent it develops its own forgiveness or accepts reality of this limitation.

The individual who avoids dependency on an imagined concept of self-congratulation or forgiveness develops a deeper sense of self, and at the same time advances sophistication of the species in which it exists. Inasmuch as each new species is recognized as advanced from a previous one, it could be accepted that any increase in understanding and sophistication of the individual is consequently replicated in any species to follow. This might suggest the child would be more advanced than the parent.

Inhibitors claimed as elements of a wall of ignorance are found in various social forms established to protect the individual from harm and disables the economy of its development. If confronting the inhibitor is too costly, that is, it extracts un-replenished energy in exchange for overcoming the limiting nature of the wall, the potential for understanding, and thence growth of the individual, is limited. This "social contract" between self and a protective shield against limiting ignorance at the hands of the State optimizes the continuity of the physical being but at the same time restricts its ability to understand itself as unique within its environment.

The freedom an individual seeks in living is the ability to experience and to learn from his/her environment, specifically in perpetuating growth in understanding self, without encumbrance of artificial or imposed restrictions from walls of ignorance.

The role of freedom in democracy

From the Code of Hammurabi in approximately 2,000 BCE comes separation of classes of individuals along three lines: property owners, free men, slaves. Degree of freedom is granted through parameters of class, such that specific benefits are available only within classes, with upper classes benefitting from a hierarchy of freedoms granted above lower classes.

In rejecting the notion of class, the U.S. Declaration of Independence in 1776 defined for all Americans the extent of freedoms such as Life, Liberty and the pursuit of Happiness. Thomas Paine's Rights of Man served as inspiration for freedom to the revolutionary American states, and was also published by France's National Constituent Assembly in 1791 as "Declaration of Rights of the Man" and later for the "Citizen of the French Republic" in 1798 from its own revolution to obtain freedom.[51]

John Locke (1632-1704) believed that freedom in human nature allowed people to be self-serving.[52] In a natural state all people are equal in one sense but independent, and everyone has a natural right to defend his "life, health, liberty, or possession." One might imagine, following such position, that if every human were to express him/herself freely, chaos would surely result. Hence, the need for the rule of civil law under a governing body.

While it was considered obvious to the Framers at the time the U.S. Constitution was drafted, Amendment I in the 1791 Bill of Rights was required in claiming, "Congress shall make no law respecting an establishment of

---

[51] "Declaration of the Rights of the Man and of the Citizen," published by France's National Constituent Assembly in 1789, is a human civil rights document from the French Revolution.

[52] John Locke's Political Philosophy discussed at https://www.iep.utm.edu/locke-po/.

religion, or prohibiting the free exercise thereof; or abridging the freedom of speech, or of the press; or the right of the people peaceably to assemble, and to petition the government for a redress of grievances.53 But are such freedoms limited to only classless societies, and don't they come with oversight?

Is there no pushback against government actions limiting these constitutional freedoms? In the United States, "challenges to those freedoms by government officials or other actors encounter vigorous and often successful resistance from civil society, the press, the political opposition, and a judiciary which is mindful of its role as a restraint on executive and legislative excess," as reported in the Washington Times as recently as 2008.54 Rigorous pushback occurred in the White House of 2019 against such challenges related to continuous and uncontrolled build-up of anti-terrorist measures.

The State expresses for itself a higher priority than supporting freedoms to its citizens. It seeks to preserve its own existence before all else. This would seem self-evident if the State where considered an entity apart from the society it is responsible for protecting. Unless society fearing loss of freedoms at the hands of a power-seeking State takes action against totalitarianism, as advised by John Locke, the State acting as a single entity with its own self-interested sovereignty is the only entity to enjoy the benefits of freedom.

---

[53] United States Bill of Rights, 1791.

[54] "Today's American: How Free?" Freedom House, as reported in The Washington Times, May 4, 2008.

A simple truth

Freedom is a faulty objective if misunderstood. It leads to acceptance of human principles operating to prefer give and take, to show how loss and gain operate together. A democracy is rule-based, depending on the result of power determining direction for society at the hands of the State. Freedoms of some deny by circumstance freedoms of others so that tendency for balance is sought. Balance trumps freedom. The citizen is left to determine for him/herself what constitutes appropriate balance.

How might the meaning of freedom be regulated, as required in a democratic society? Common perspective must exist before government action can be relevant. If government is populated by elected leaders at the pleasure of a voting public, one might expect the voting public to reflect a common concept of freedom. Among themselves, citizens should participate in discussion and debate addressing potential loss and gain, based on a common perspective of what freedom means - today as much as was intended historically. For that reason, the Public Sphere is an appropriate venue.

Fundamental to any perception of freedom is self. Each of us wants to be free to assure well being in our own life. In order to avoid damage from rule-less chaos, absence of concern for the individual, we accept some level of behavioral control. That level should not be determined by self interests of the individual but must be set based on what all of society, or a majority of it, determines is appropriate in the service the State provides within limits of oppression from its oversight of the individual.

Dialogue 5. Knowledge as Capital

Understandably, society insists on a well-informed populace to support valid democracy. Thomas Jefferson made this point clear in his letter to Richard Price in 1789.[55] Anchors of American democracy were being set in various documents claiming need for citizens to be well informed, which is to say, knowledgeable of political needs. Application of knowledge must be understood in order to appreciate the value in Jefferson's point. Possession of knowledge means little if action is not associated with it.

And so, we experience great insistence that a basis of knowledge is made requirement for every voting citizen in a democracy. Through public schools, various forms of free press, public forums, and today through social networks, every citizen can expect that at least potential for developing a base for knowledge exists and that it should be pursued in order to support responsive democracy.

Does access to information result in acquisition of knowledge? To recall the words of John Dewey, and reflecting on Plato's Problem, information can lead to theory, but knowledge requires experience. What can be said about transforming information to knowledge in the absence of experience or participation?

---

[55] Thomas Jefferson letter to Richard Price, Paris, January 8, 1789. Found at https://founders.archives.gov/documents/Jefferson/01-14-02-0196

Developing Knowledge

Living provides an opportunity to develop knowledge. An infant coming into existence has no account of knowledge, as the process of knowing must be developed, or taught, through experiencing information. (Physical characteristics may be inherited from parents, but knowledge is not.) During a lifetime of one individual, knowledge is developed and retained or forgotten. But this knowledge, in total, is lost when the individual dies. How then is it transmitted in order to retain value for total society which outlives the individual?

Still, society in surviving the individual is the embodiment of knowledge. One generation of society differs from a preceding one in the amount of knowledge transferred iteratively from the former to the latter. The nature of this knowledge requires investigation.

Societies result from groups of like-minded individuals who believe in the need to develop and retain a means to survive and grow, and that special qualification for this behavior rests with its members and only with its members. Earlier examples of the Illuminati, followed by secret dealings of the Knights Templar during and briefly following the many Crusades, then by Masons, to modern day groups such as the notorious Scull and Bones society at Yale University, all demonstrate that such societies come into existence for the purpose of guarding knowledge and passing it on to future generations, even if their populations are exclusively limited. How these groups survive across generations is a different issue to consider.

Societies seek to survive, much as humans do. We see this behavior in any large group, even groups of bureaucracies developed to govern larger societies. Bureaucracies control resources, therefor survival is subject to two influences: internal attempts to protect, and external to satisfy demand for services.56

Closed societies in small groups might seek protection from more open ones when there is common interest among its members to participate. That is, if the goals of any society, even a secret society, anticipate shared values, a mutually supportive complementation could expect to result. This also applies to a government society. Embodiment of what is claimed to be knowledge is embodied in documents and then preserved.

A difference in the base of knowledge developed and retained by a secret group in alliance with the larger, protective government group, constitutes what is categorized as elitism. The need for secrecy can be seen in how selectivity and need to protect identity restricts membership. Perception of threat from the elite would seem natural by those being excluded from receiving benefits given only to members of the secret society and restricted to them.

We might claim government leaders are not appropriately held accountable for their behaviors, but we misdirect concern. Government leaders might indeed be accountable, but to a different source of power. This different society is the quasi-secret one whose contributions to government in order to survive are considered of greater value than the popular vote. Claims of importance for the popular vote are necessary only for the appearance of a citizen power base. In actuality, importance of the bureaucratic function is determined by officials with membership in discrete secret societies, whether or not they are elected by the public.

---

56 Discussed by Alexander Matejko in "*The Obsolescence of Bureaucracy*," Industrial Relations, Vol. 35, No. 3 (467-493) 1980.

What is the knowledge transferred in such arrangement, that is, what value to a base of social knowledge results from a closed, even secret, relationship between an elitist society and a protective government? At the base of the question lies another question. Is the desire for development and retention of any base of knowledge an indication that a state of perfection is possible for the elitist society, that then creates an even more elite and influential society to assure legitimacy? Would it be any wonder, therefore, that welfare of those members of the larger public fearing government control would be dismissed as an unimportant contributor to knowledge building?

As government increasingly takes on characteristics of the special society providing them value (quid pro quo), might it also be reasonable that members of both societies (secret and government) be one and the same? Are members of government who relinquish positions of power to an elite social segment concerned at all for having found a different sponsorship than from voter support?

Elite elements benefit from favorable influence from government policy implemented during their respective existence. Who would control the capital of knowledge if it is limited to the secret group, and whose access to its power would be protected by government regulations resulting from policies that support elite source?

Yet, democracy for the people may still survive

There is no claimed value in, nor need for, knowledge described from any document supporting government action in support of the larger society. Such content is static, and constrained by legal phrasing with historical relevance. Existence of knowledge as claimed by Thomas Jefferson, or by liberal political thinkers after the Enlightenment, is freely developed, enriched as occurs from experience in time. What qualifies as knowledge depends on how it is developed and in what manner it is used. If Jefferson was correct, that a well informed populace is necessary to "set the government right," care is needed in examining the knowledge base that informs the populace.

But, can democracy result from a populace either not informed or ill-informed? So long as people are free to influence the form and process of government, can one but claim that democracy is in place. Democracy, it might be argued, may not result from a knowledge base which does not support government behaving in a way that serves its own survival but does not support its citizens. Knowledge base for government is different from the knowledge base of citizens. What supports citizens may depend on other than how knowledge represents them, if their source of information supporting knowledge is unfit to those who fix the rules of government.

A simple truth

Democracy does not depend on policy support to the elite. After all, the elite depends on static conditions of security and preservation. Nature provides neither. Nature's value is found in how knowledge is developed and not in the manner it is preserved for the sake of a self serving governing society claiming to be protective.

Knowledge is not circumstantial. Nor is it absolute. What is lacking in determining degrees of any knowledge is awareness of the reality supporting its existence. Any knowledge claimed by an institution's hierarchy suffers from lack of awareness of those who experience it and what roles in life the individual performs in gaining that experience.

How valuable to democracy is a knowledge base derived from dialog at the citizen level? Federal processes often reflect disconnect from local interests. Protests and riots from discontent happen. Should they occur at local levels, at county or state levels, or in a venue for consideration by the total population? Vietnam provided a good example for protests claimed against effectiveness at the federal level, but what was expected to result from the protests that actually did not? Fighting in Vietnam was terminated, but the issue of military engagement without civilian support did not.

How then could the process favoring interests in the Public Sphere move upward in the governmental hierarchy? They must begin at the lower level, and elected officials should be held accountable to that level for supporting them from their higher level. As these individually born issues move up the hierarchy they meet possible conflicting values presented at each level by groups of other community voices. New majorities are formed. Hence, support from overall democracy itself is diminished by the self-serving process it claims is supportive to the individual. Changing pluralism can be disruptive to personal choice outside the mainstream of politics.

Is the Public Sphere appropriate solely in itself for adequate knowledge transfer, to identify and discuss issues? How could results of knowledge transfer reach higher policy levels for consideration by policy makers? Communication must be vertical to include government as the latter is developed horizontally at the pleasure of public discourse.

Of course, one might suggest, as Douglas Adams did, that the universe and everything it contain is knowable by virtue of its mere existence.[57] A search for knowledge may not exist properly in developing linear sequence between cause and effect, observation and logical explanation. As the public is capable of arguing when addressing phenomena of the unknown, whatev-

---

[57] See Adams, Douglas, Hitchhiker's Guide to the Galaxy, Pan Books, 1979.

er exists is better explained through examining first what is perceived as the answer, followed by rationalizations of its causality.

Dialogue 6. Value in Difference

For centuries, and virtually everywhere in the world, civic expressions of inequality have focused on insufficient respect for women and general treatment depriving them of the opportunity to help form society, and more particularly against participation as leaders in the governments that serve societies.

Free Press Unlimited describes "different access to resources, including information and opportunities, and ability to make choices about their lives is rooted in existing norms that define expectations and beliefs about men's and women's roles in society."58 Variance in roles for the two genders is found in different classes, ethnic groups, and in other social and cultural divides.

Considering that across the many years of human existence males have controlled the formative roles influencing rules of society, how could anyone dispute a claim that the world is created by men for men? While we shouldn't discount responsibility of the male to support the well being of the female, the relationship has depended on how the male views society and nature of the female rather than determination through equal perspective by both genders.

Many females may choose to accept that leadership roles should be held by the male, but is choice a fair element to claim preference determined merely from acceptance? We might accept that partnership between males

---

58 Free Press Unlimited, found at https://www.freepressunlimited.org/sites/freepressunlimited.org/files/gender_equality_policy_building_inclusive_societies_in_and_through_the_media.pdf

and females is a better focus than accepting either gender as principle designer of social responsibilities.59 But a too heavy focus on the issue of equality brings bias to the issue, as Friedan later demonstrated.60 Balance is claimed appropriate, but how can balance be determined if the starting point emphasizes male dominance? Such determination provides an unfair disadvantage for females.

Should gender roles really be equal?

Many disputes can be encountered by claiming lack of equal rights for minorities, or even majorities in the case of women. No matter how any population is characterized by elements of difference, less advantaged sides claim unfair treatment for themselves.

Although arguments of natural disadvantage in some activities result from gender difference, most public rhetoric occurs in how a conservative society focusing on status quo treats gender difference - as distinguished from sex - as a non-choice issue. In any debate, female rights are pitted against an established bias favoring males. Both levels of achievement and compensation for effort are claimed to have placed females in an unfavorable socio-economic position.

Why do women make claim for rights found among men? Is there in implicit assertion that women and men should be treated as if they are the same in all respects? - or even if they are equal, functionally? Look carefully at behavioral characteristics and try to claim equality between men and women. Is there not a clear distinction to be made between asserting need

---

[59] Friedan, Betty, The Feminine Mystique. W.W. Norton and Co, 1963.

[60] Friedan, Bette, The Second Stage. Summit Books, 1981.

for domestic stability from maternal instinct and physical requirement for economic and physical security? Since no such correlation is perfect, at least to the extent that correlation should not imply cause and effect, men can be found with varying levels of strong home caring behavior, and women can demonstrate varying levels of effective skills at assuring economic and physical safety. Whether or not they do so is a different matter.

Several points should be clear. Structure of society in today's world is determined by male-dominated behavior.61 As in other elements of nature, reproductive and behavioral strategies between genders lead to distinct sexual segregation. In effect, women who claim unfair social and economic treatment argue they should be treated as men in a world designed by and in support of male behavior. Although one gender can demonstrate facility for behaving as if it were the other gender, such characteristic indicates similarity rather than congruence in intent. That is, gender behavioral crossover remains more socially abnormal than normal.

Returning to the distinction between gender and sex, it isn't at all clear that the two should be regarded as synonymous. Gender is an element of nature from which arguments associating reproductive behavior and choice in sexual participation appear. Sex is behavioral. While male and female gender difference can be noted in the fetus, conflating the character of maleness and femaleness at that early stage, later behavioral difference among the genders results from social elements.

What then can be determined of value if the female quality is introduced into a world dominated by male design? How could shift in contemporary

---

61 See perspective of William L. Mace in "Male Dominance in Public Life," Psychology Today, 2019, found at https://www.psychologytoday.com/us/blog/campus-confidential-coping-college/201901/male-dominance-in-public-life.

inequality be most effective in democratic society? One can look at the nature of politics and how political behavior can be applied for the sake of a society that claims to assure domestic tranquility (both family and society), economic stability, and peaceful international relations.

Two other points are addressed. The world (small or large elements) continues to change - necessarily, inasmuch as stability in nature seems not to have an achievable endpoint. Secondly, any normative democracy features determination for leadership in government from the people. The latter condition reflects both male and female perspectives, behaviors, and purposeful values. Thus, citizens must determine, through their own participation, how society must adjust to changing conditions.

Careful review of society's conformance with nature demonstrates periods during which stability in domestic issues such as family, national and domestic economic, and national and international security are assured. Elements demonstrated by each gender individually seem required in assuring stability for these issues. And, either of the genders can demonstrate capability.

Structure of government contains frequent periodicity of change. Leadership in government should not be considered a long-term nor professional class in which representation by individuals could result in government unable to adjust to change. Effective government would refocus itself based on challenges from fluid domestic, economic, and safety issues.

Outfitting government with elements of both male and female leadership qualities, over short intervals of time, better assures long-term stability as it aligns with changes in nature, and procedurally removes any element of unequal or biased treatment of either gender.

The problem of gender inequality perpetuated in democracy

We return to the age of the constitutional framers to see how democracy then was structured around the male. Responsibilities of females were not overlooked by many early statesmen, but females occupied only secondary roles in which they were considered supported by their husband leaders. We note as example the case of letters from President John Adams applauding his wife Abigail for support to intellectual discussions on government and politics.62 But discussers are not necessarily decision-makers.

Almost a hundred years later, the first female candidate for president appeared on the scene. Victoria Woodhull ran for U.S. President as an Equal Rights candidate.63 Although she was not taken seriously as a candidate - perhaps because she was on the ticket with abolitionist leader Frederick Douglass, she did make a name for herself through her encouragement toward equal social rights and labor reform.

Some years later, the United States experienced the 19th Amendment to the Constitution providing voting rights to women. This came after another wife, that of President Wilson, attempted from a poor base of awareness of political matters to pre-empt influence from Colonel House, a male confi-

---

62 See many of these discussions at https://www.masshist.org/digitaladams/archive/letter/

63 Victoria Woodhull was a leader of the women's movement, along with the leadership of Susan B. Anthony and Elizabeth Cady Stanton beginning in 1848 at Seneca Falls, New York. In 1872, she ran for President as an Equal Rights candidate.

dent of the President.64 In doing so, she lost favor as a female partner confidante but at least weakened the dependency of the President on advice from other male political associates.

The struggle for gender equality continues today, seemingly anchored in elements created by males for determination of what constitutes government under the current form of democracy. This ideal claims equal rights but in practice reflects the male imprint on both form and method.

A simple truth

Rather than consider difference between genders and then attempt to equalize treatment for either to demonstrate fairness, characteristic of difference should form a basis for how the separate genders arrive at complementation. In that way, elements of difference can be found from each gender to result in fairness defined by and benefiting from these elements to serve all of society.

From the perspective of democracy, there is no female who does not contain citizenship elements of the male, and vice versa. The difference for democracy is only in the degree one gender is represented in legislation compared with the other.

Any perspective on the issue should evolve from a forum that includes women in the first place. Public gatherings should not be limiting such that men talk to men and women talk to women. It is at this juncture of mixed genders that attitudes toward any political issue could originate, and should thus reflect the seeds for equality. Equality would be based not uniquely on

---

64 Discussed by Judith L. Weaver in "Edith Bolling Wilson as First Lady: A Study in the Power of Personality, 1919-1920," Presidential Studies Quarterly, (Winter, 1985), pp. 51-76.

difference in nature but performance in the Public Sphere. Among the many attitudes individuals can express, those discussed to arrive at deeper understanding by sharing what is experienced lead to agreement on the role of genders: individually and together.

Dialogue 7. Energy from Wisdom

It might occur to citizens in a democracy that electing officials represents creation of a form of energy for government that legitimizes itself through results from perpetual practice. Voting is a form of electoral energy. It operates through transfer of power to elected representatives. From there it can result in effective productivity for the benefit of citizens, or it can result in another form of Karma that manipulates or competitively exists as a power-grab.

In democracy as a location of power from voting we expect service to provide care and comfort to the populace. It is new form of energy (service) derived from a former energy source (voting) to elect officials from electors. Einstein described this in 1905 with his e=mc2 equation. Energy is not created; it is transformed from one source to another.

Matter and energy: *depuis, en face de la cheminée*[65]

Wood combusts when sufficient heat is present to cause the release of gas. The gas then combusts, generating sufficient heat itself to perpetuate the flame, until no more matter remains in the form of combustible material. Matter is transformed to gas, gas to matter. Transformation occurs in the presence of energy. At what point would there be no energy loss when gas combusts? It merely changes form.

In other words, wood continues to release energy in the presence of heat until the amount of heat is no longer adequate to cause released gas. Over time, wood no longer possesses potential for energy transfer to support

---

[65] While in front of the fireplace

combustion. For its part, gas will continue to combust as it is heated until the point where it develops its own heat. When does this point occur, assuming it does? It occurs when there is no longer a source of energy to support combustion.

In other words, heated matter beyond its kindling point transforms to gas and then combusted through energy exchange. Heat is regenerated in a process with an endpoint. When matter no longer supports transformation through heat to gas, gas no longer has access to sufficient energy to perpetuate its own existence. Heat energy produced by burning gas is no longer supported.

When the heat generated by combusted gas results in a level of heat greater than that produced by the combusting wood, one observes an opposite of entropy. Rather than level of energy dissipating from matter becoming consumed by combustion, the level of energy from the burning gas released by the wood increases rather than decreases over time. What results is a form of perpetual energy, with only changes in form.

Energy of democratic government

So it is with a democratic government. Energy expressed through voting is transformed into the energy of governance. Government by virtue of its having been created proceeds to replicate itself while producing energy of governance.

One might suppose that resulting energy of government takes a form that represents voting intent. This intent results either from voting energy or from government reacting to itself. While the latter can be categorized as systematic by constitutional design, energy from voting follows a different path. The electoral path may not be unidirectional, by design, as different perspectives of intent are present in each occurrence of voting behavior.

Investigation is invited toward influences on voting. Political ideology, the essence of rational voting behavior, might seem to have an anchor in morality, but morality lacks a single creating element.

We observe that morality represents the individual belief system of voters. That is, each voter represents a different morality based on what he/she believes. Conflict naturally results. Even if common elements can be found at the base of expressions of morality fundamentally, each voter casts choice behind a veil of ignorance characterized by John Rawls.66

In what way can wisdom as an energy that supports voting provide an explanation of increase in effective democracy? Does explanation for results of voting exist whether or not most favorable political choice is understood by voters? Is attaining wisdom for voting the process of experiencing value developed from understanding how voting resulted in past government performance? Or, does it result from a form of knowledge influenced artificially from expediency or by targeted marketing from special interest or misinforming media?

A distorted focus of voting, following peculiarities of individual voters, might suggest movement toward entropy - the valueless result of a democratic process merely to keep voters involved. If reversing entropy is desired, that is, providing wisdom from energy formed from understanding processes to support voting, would explanation of growth in the energy of government be demonstrated, a priori? Is a new energy, resulting from informed voting process behavior a pure increase created by transformation rather than from

---

66 Discussed in Under-used Tools for Conflict Resolution,
Barry Anderson, Les Swanson, and Sam Imperati.

the mere act of voting? Can wisdom result from other than the energy needed to vote, that is, from knowledge or awareness? Could this wisdom pre-exist as an element of nature?

As in a flame from combusting wood, can a new source of energy result from transforming energy arrived through informed voting, such as for democracy? Does the energy in government performance reduce by lack of support or does it increase the potential energy of the voter who remains informed and involved?

A simple truth

Wisdom results from energy developed from knowledge. The basis for knowledge depends on what is understood. Wisdom can therefore represent falseness, to the extent what is understood is misaligned with reality. Human weakness lacking understanding of life, governmental politics and the integral role of the individual contributes to falseness. Awareness leading to wisdom comes from investigation of perceptions from different viewers. Debate provides the catalyst for such energy development, but first there must be discussion. Discussion exposes the energy of intent. In so doing, intent forms a basis unto itself as an energy source. Building proper intent is an objective of any debate during discussion. When intent represents the view of a majority, the resulting political action is fully representative, and elected officials have a more valid base for developing policy, to the extent they pay attention to the energy from voters.

Dialogue 8. Spinoza had it right; but with what consequence?

A perspective exists in regards to American democracy which reflects individualism. The claim is that each individual is unique, and that government should treat individuals as such.

Spinoza claimed that individuals are the source of a power that resides innately. It is the basic form of existence.[67] Americans as individuals can live their "dream" only as individuals. Any individual can become president, or so it is claimed. Any person working hard deserves all the benefits life has to offer. This is perhaps too singular a perspective.

A broader perspective for humanity is to consider the individual as a functioning element of a larger system, the system of humanity worldwide. The individual does not serve only the self, but serves the collective element of humanity representative of the entire world's population.

For those with a world-view, or for those who have at least some sensitivity toward events worldwide, the question, "Why?" seems relevant. Why are things as they are, or at least as they appear to be? Beyond a filtered view from within the United States life outside seems unrealistically harsh.

Perhaps a view other than brutality in humans exists, apologies to Thomas Hobbes. Attention to other things than human brutality might focus better on events causing pain and suffering. No doubt the media is partly to

---

[67] "Individuation by essence" in Spinoza's Physical Theory, Stanford Encyclopedia of Philosophy. See also, Manning, Richard, "Spinoza's Physical Theory", *The Stanford Encyclopedia of Philosophy* (Winter 2016 Edition), Edward N. Zalta (ed.), URL = <https://plato.stanford.edu/archives/win2016/entries/spinoza-physics/>

blame, perhaps in large part. While one can feel sorrow and regret for pain and suffering portrayed in news of events beyond national boundaries, nature itself demonstrates a broader distribution of the same elements of pain. As humans we should be concerned by causes of these elements. We seem to not know why they occur. They are not discussed in the Public Sphere.

The means for knowing

From Spinoza we learn that humans understand knowing in three stages: uncertainty or imagination is experienced; reasoning follows empirically; ultimately an awareness of God takes hold.68 This gradation implies a direction of maturity in understanding as different stages are experienced. Many would suspect that most of humanity is found at the lowest stage. (Some individuals might claim naively that the third stage could occur without the benefit of the experience stage.) We act on the basis of probability at that third stage, and not at too sophisticated a level.

Imagine that the telephone rings. Who is calling? We don't really know without evidence such as Caller Id on the device, but even then how certain can we be in believing who is on the other end of the call? It's Sunday afternoon and mother calls around this time. Is mother the caller on this occasion? If we had to bet, how much is a guess worth? How much expense for loss can be linked with a wrong guess?

Is Iran developing, or in the process of developing, a nuclear weapon? Evidence exists that elements are in place to claim the positive. Other evidence suggests that no intention toward nuclear development exists? Possibly maybe, but not highly probable.

---

68 Found in G. H. R. Parkinson, *Spinoza's Theory of Knowledge*. (Oxford: Clarendon Press, 1954).

For governments promoting an international policy for no more nuclear arms development, putting aside any self-serving value of such policy, how much should be invested to minimize any risk that Iran has, indeed, the intention of developing nuclear weapons? The justification for any preemptive behavior should of course be based on knowledge - that Iran is or is not developing nuclear weapons. Alas, foreign policy makers find themselves at Spinoza's lowest stage, a low probability of being correct, a high correlated probability of actually being wrong. All manner of justification can occur to explain how risk, even if in error, could be ameliorated.

Returning to causes of human pain and suffering, are causes natural or man-made? Putting nature aside for the moment, we look at human decisions created or caused by some level of knowledge.

Are decisions based on likelihood, empirical evidence, or on primal causes from God? How much effort would be necessary for humanity to move from likelihood into information collection and evaluation to arrive at least at Spinoza's second stage? We leave it to philosophers to identify causation, but shouldn't there be a little philosophical orientation in each of us?

Could it be that levels of knowing correlate highly with levels of existence for the individual in an evolutionary sense? Are we really only at Spinoza's first stage? Is it too soon in an evolutionary sense to expect humans to justify their actions and beliefs based on evidence?

Evidence of Democracy

Justice Potter Stewart famously claimed when determining what is or is not pornography, "I know it when I see it."69 Evidence of democracy seems to exist the same way. If democracy in the United States is hailed as the model for the rest of the world, yet is ranked as a failed democracy by the UK's Economist Intelligence Unit,70 what causes the misalignment in view? With such ambiguity surrounding what is or is not democracy for the United States, Spinoza's level of uncertainty or imagination seems to characterize the level of knowledge about what exists as democracy.

Justice Potter's suggestion might apply to a plurality opinion in the United States, full of conflicts. Challenged voting rights and questionable treatment of minorities could qualify at Spinoza's second level of knowledge had there not been a lack of empirical evidence to support the higher claim for democracy in the United States, at least in 2020.

What does this mean? Has the growth of democracy through legitimate behavior of citizens been the creation of a form of energy resulting in a government that serves its own purpose rather than in respecting the justifying political energy evident in 1789?

---

[69] Justice Potter in, *Jacobellis v. Ohio*, 378 U.S. 184 (1964).

[70] Democracy Index 2018, The Economist Intelligence Unit. January 2019.

A simple truth

The closest humanity can come to understanding truth results from application of what is believed, empirically. If the individual were to draw upon a different source for understanding, there would remain a need to demonstrate its applicability to truth in order for it to contribute to reality. How one arrives at this seemingly magical moment of clarity is through sharing of common thoughts about ideals and processes. There is much to discuss in the Public Sphere, especially in sharing experience as a source of understanding.

Dialogue 9. Questions about Meaning

With so much uncertainty in the process of government around the world, could there be refuge in forms of democracy? The question has no reasonable answer considering how meaning for democracy seems undetermined, other than vague reference to "value for citizens." In this limitation of meaning for democracy there is little room to consider as valid any other specific process of governing that functions well to support citizen needs. This rules out aristocracy, totalitarianism, and oligarchy, in favor of government formed by the voice of the people, for the benefit of the people.

Robert Dahl claims that for more than a century democracy has triumphed over all other forms of anti-democratic government.71 He reports that regimes such as communism and fascism have disappeared. Two problems result from this assertion. One is that both elements of communism and fascism can be found in governments today claimed as democratic. The second is that democracy ranges in application from despotic administrations such as found in Russia to political control of democratic processes in place in China.

What's it all about?

Based on criteria posed by The Economist Intelligence Unit, evaluating measurable degrees of democracy, five categories should be considered: electoral process and pluralism; civil liberties; the functioning of government; political participation; and political culture.72 None if these cate-

---

71 Robert A. Dahl, On Democracy. Yale University Press, 2000.

72 Democracy Index 2018, The Economist Intelligence Unit. January 2019.

gories has unique meaning specific to democracy. Varying amounts of each can be found in any form of a society controlled by government. Expert assessment is needed for measuring the categories, and this suggests at the heart of any assessment lies interpretation of meaning.

It is not infrequent that we hear the question, What does that mean? Indeed! What is meaning? Is meaning free of content, based largely on how information is perceived? Is "the medium the message?" Is it relative to a specific element rather than existing as a standalone condition? Should information be believed to have no absolute meaning, requiring relevance?

Does a dream or an ideal have meaning? If so, what gives it meaning. Is the meaning in a dream or an ideal imposed by memory of past events or recent experiences? Or does meaning derive from something innate to the dreamer to signal pre-existing content?

Does an idea reflect unique meaning? What source exists for any idea? Who deserves credit for an idea? Can the idea be owned? Is the basis for historical meaning found in the expression of an idea of its existence at a specific time?

Is it possible to have the same idea twice? That is, once an idea is expressed, reflecting original meaning, does restatement of the same idea gain uniqueness on its own? Or does it replicate or credit the idea in its original form? Can there be uniqueness in an idea if it can occur twice?

If the question of meaning is absurd, why does it exist? Since it does exist, why does it lack value for any discussion of it? Shouldn't there be investigation of meaning for any expression of information?

Why search for meaning? Is there a basic lack of security in communication that mistrust demands investigation of meaning? Meaning reflects existence of something specific, even unique, a single entity at the center of understanding of each thing knowable.

Ideal or behavior

Virtually all definitions for meaning of democracy include, along with attention to citizen participation in election of leaders, provisions for how the government behaves. One might ask whether this refers to overall government, such as parliamentary or presidential government, or institutions of government, such as executive or legislative.

Considering legislative, it might be reasonable to consider what is being claimed as important as voters select representative members. If interests of local jurisdictions, or even states or municipalities found in other governments, are being represented in the legislature, has republicanism transformed meaning in representation from the citizen to the larger political entity reflecting a majority? In this way, representation of the majority is not of the individual citizen; it is of groups of citizens. Degree of dependance on meaning for how the majority reflects values of the individual determines behavior of an institution reflecting the actualized meaning of democracy.

One might claim that representation of whatever political entity is being represented is reflected by the ability of the elected individual to accomplish the desired behavior. In this regard, professionalism is questioned. Professionalism could refer to the manner in which an official determines need and in finding means to address it. Or, professionalism could refer to the acquisition of talent after having gained proficiency over time, enough proficiency to accommodate desires of constituency no matter what they happen to be. In the latter case of professionalism, what is the meaning of representation if representatives form something other than constituency choice to influence meaning?

In considering the executive in a leadership role, is it possible that representation reflects choice of a majority of individual members of a total population? If not, and there would be no justification in claiming otherwise, why should election of the executive rest in the hands of individual voters? Voters in groups reflecting a majority would have more relevant meaning.

Humans do not function in an environment limited to what individuals know. What does exist is what groups with influential power determine as relevant. Actions of groups give meaning to government. Shouldn't democracy reflect more the actions of government serving interests of groups than merely supporting demands of individual voters? Influence of voters cannot equal that of groups of financial contributors. Should it be claimed that sources of wealth influence the nature of democracy?

Worldwide support for democracy remains strong, according to a recent Pew poll,73 although great dissatisfaction with democracy is reported by alternative forms of government. Preference for democracy among non-democracy States seems a vote for something other than exists in place. Voting for difference is hardly a legitimate support for democracy even if poll numbers indicate otherwise.

A more refined poll, one limited to local interest and opinion, might produce different results. Local interests are more appropriate to determining effective governance for citizens than a collective voice of centralized gov-

---

[73] "Public Trust in Government: 1958-2019," Pew Research Center, found at https://www.people-press.org/2019/04/11/public-trust-in-government-1958-2019/

ernment.74 One might suspect that among local areas low in the hierarchy of government levels great variance in citizen expectations could result. Is central government supportive of local interests? What form of governance would realign negative concerns with the overall democracy? That might suggest layers for democracy, something similar to a program instituted in support of local groups along lines of the now extinct Articles of Confederation where State power was preeminent to central government power.75 The growth of support for local government since then, and most recently during the Administration of Ronald Reagan under a policy of Federalism,76 has been more pronounced in how local authority can execute programs more effectively in support of specific local needs.

A simple truth

Perhaps local power should have greater relevance in supporting local interests than through central government programs for Block Grants and special Entitlement Grants. High tradeoff interest in national security and comprehensive economic stability could be compromised. What better means to examine the issue than to energize the Public Sphere and to let supported opinions resonate upward with elected federal policy officials. David Hume might be well pleased.

---

74 Discussed by David Hume in "Idea of a Perfect Commonwealth" (1777) found at https://oll.libertyfund.org/pages/oll-reader-70

75 See discussion of the Articles of Confederation at https://history.state.gov/milestones/1776-1783/articles.

76 Discussed at https://www.reaganlibrary.gov/presketch-1

Dialogue 10. Pandora for Democracy

Building myths seems a natural tendency for human beings. Collectively, myths represent the view of the human regarding life and its mysteries. Myths function very much as Plato considered an ideal. As one learns to worship something outside the real, it is revered. Only, there are so many myths. Might we develop a hierarchy of them, such that the myths one culture accepts are more valid, or more meaningful, than those of another culture? Such hierarchy could be built, for example, around aging as indicator of advanced maturity, or gender that supports the male as master of social behavior, or by ranking of special groups organized around elite principles.77

No matter how we choose to categorize things, we tend to collapse them into dichotomies: good and bad, black and white, up and down.

Prometheus brought us fire (the good things) against the wishes of the elite and powerful among all Gods; Pandora according to Hesiod brought us the opposite things, the punishment for Prometheus's error, according to the Greeks.78

The creation of Pandora was not first with Hesiod; other myths demonstrating the dichotomy of good and bad preceded Hesiod. One can note the same mythical character of innocent Eve influenced by Satan as evil in the Bible as the appearance of original sin. Somewhere in the consciousness of

---

[77] See Sidanius J, Cotterill S, Sheehy-Skeffington J, Kteily N, Carvacho H. Social dominance theory: explorations in the psychology of oppression, In Press.

[78] Discussed at https://www.greekmythology.com/Myths/Mortals/Pandora/pandora.html

humans arises the sense that some difference should be acknowledged between what is and what should be.

In what way should we understand difference between what is and what should be? How could we? Even if we should and could, what useful guidance for determining belief would result? Could we then say something is either right or wrong, evil or angelic? Is that why religion claims a God in Heaven is good and a Devil in Hell is bad? Is there no way to see life, or the process of existence, as a natural embodiment of both?

The good and bad of democracy

As a quote credited to Winston Churchill suggests, democracy is the worst form of government that has existed, except for all others.79 As an ideal this may be true, considering that democracy fundamentally is reliable in cycles that determine its behavior, dependent on delivered results from its processes, and supportive to voting citizens who participate in determining electoral outcomes for leadership based on trust in sovereign guidance.

Democracy appears to benefit from strength of claims by voting citizens it is designed to support. Through exercised rights of choice, the ideal reflects the means to self-adjust to fix problematic unanticipated issues. This suggest a possible liability in that democracy is susceptible to change to the extent its government does not continue to react reliably.

On the negative side of democracy, just because an official is elected, it does not mean that the individual newly in power would remain faithful to the mandate throughout the duration of term in office. The element of change is inevitable in any administration, potentially creating a basis of

---

[79] Quotation from International Churchill Society, found at https://winstonchurchill.org/resources/quotes/the-worst-form-of-government/

disapproval by those whose choice reflects circumstances prior to the change. If democracy were not amenable to change, it could not adjust its own behavior to accommodate new requirements, even as it would tend to fall in disfavor for some.

At the time of this writing, the British Parliament was in the throes of determining how best to reflect a referendum determination of citizens who wanted the country to severe its relationship with the European Union. (Set aside the reasons for believing such claim.) The House of Commons in the British democratic Parliament had been trying to find the most favorable means of assuring this termination.

Due largely to legal matters complicating the attempt, no acceptable method had resulted after more than two years of deliberation. In the process, conditions for negotiating separation had been modified to reflect legal requirements imposed by the European Union as a higher body and to compromise demands interpreted by voters. The resulting position ran afoul of European authority and demonstrated major economic problems in the original mandate. One might note from the conflict between British citizens, their Parliament and the European Union that the standoff in the Parliament did not satisfy the desires of the ruling party, and was also different from original expectations from the referendum.80

What was represented in the behavior of the legislative body? Support to the people, support to the regions represented by members of the House of Commons, or only perspective of the Prime Minister who authored an unfavorable proposal for separation? In particular, what is being represented, the

---

[80] The Brexit process is mostly accomplished, as reflected in "Post-Brexit Guide: Where are we now – and how did we get here?" Euronews. 6 May, 2020, updated at https://www.euronews.com/2020/02/11/brexit-draft-deal-first-of-many-hurdles-to-a-smooth-exit

citizens, the Parliament, or the Prime Minister, or even by extension, the European Union?

To those claiming democracy to be the culprit in the conflict, the process seemed to be more at fault than the ideal. But if the resulting process is at fault, what value exists in the ideal? To those claiming democracy as an ineffectual form of government, examples exist of corruption, demagoguery and takeovers by authoritarian individuals seeking to promote their own positions rather than those of the electorate. Others point to a tendency to support demands of the majority in a form of mob rule, while others insist that too much attention through democracy has been devoted to supporting the minority at the expense of economic stability.

Neither examples of anarchy nor mob rule as behavioral characteristic fits the overall ideal claimed for a democracy designed to reflect public choice. In practice, utopian ideals never work. Why then is so much attention devoted to spreading democracy around the world as an ideal?

The Brookings Institute characterized a Democracy Promotion Paradox in which difficulties from "numerous inconsistencies and paradoxes" between theory and practice of promoting democracy occur, at least reflected in the government in the United States.81 The paradox is demonstrated by those who promote values of democracy from an incomplete understanding of what democracy means, either as ideal or in practice. Contradictory expectations for democracy exist within political party platforms in the United States today. One claims liberal policies to assure accommodation for changing circumstances while the other touts need for maintaining status

---

81 Mitchell, Lincoln A. The Democratic Promotion Paradox. Brookings Institution Press, 2016

quo - protecting "originalism" of conservative values defined at the beginning of the nation's history.82

Looking to the view of democracy by Karl Marx we find arguments on both sides of the issue.83 While Marx supported democracy as a desirable ideal from a theoretical basis,84 his resistance appears to result from how democracy was to have been practiced, economically. He also pointed out tendency for corruption in leadership, and allegiance to groups which gain power from special interest.

Value in both perspectives

Pandora, in a manner of thinking, is the opposite of Prometheus. Is there not the same degree of truth presented under each characterization? Can we not accept both as necessary elements in human thought? If Prometheus brought knowledge to humans, it seemed necessary to create mythically an opposite to bring balance to understanding existence.

So, can we say: in every bad there is good; in every good there is bad? That could satisfy most humans. But, we should acknowledge a relationship between or value for the opposites. Then we put all our energy in promoting the good and shunning the bad of the other. It might be necessary to accept that there would be no good were it not that an opposite puts it into perspective. Shouldn't energy be devoted to understanding both opposites to find

82 Discussion of the debate can be found at https://www.npr.org/2011/10/09/141188564/a-matter-of-interpretation-justices-open-up

83 See, Wolff, Richard. "Marxism and Democracy," in Rethinking Marxism. Journal of Economics, Culture & Society, Volume 12, 2000

84 Discussed in Hal Draper's article, "Marx on Democratic Forms of Government" at social-istregister.com.

valuable as if their union comprised more appropriate explanation of existence?

In Pandora, one sees the other side of things we otherwise tend to isolate uniquely as what should be. From a form of democracy operating with the view of value in arguments for and against, overall value could be determined such that the ideal could be realized through practice.

A simple truth

For a democracy operating with the view of arguments for and against any perspective, overall value for society could be demonstrated. The ideal of democracy could be realized through practice that includes accommodating contrasts rather than through dreams from pitting one side against the other. Contrast can be debated if value is perceived for either perspective and if opportunity is created from the exercise.

It might be the debate that carries value in a democracy. Our own assessment of democracy results from debates between what was thought intended and what results were perceived. The difference can be discussed in the Public Sphere. First identification of issues; then objective debate of contradictory sides; then arrival at points to be expressed to officials responsible for following through on voter choice. From results of opening Pandora come understanding of democracy.

Dialogue 11. Be Prepared

Nuclear disarmament is a two-edged sword. Supporters are pitted against those who don't accept existence of nuclear weapons. Those who don't find value in possessing nuclear weapons are beset with an inherent fear of being over-powered by those political entities already suited with the best and most powerful nuclear capability.

Effective since 1970, the non-proliferation agreement of the United Nations provides a measure of assurance that at least partial worldwide annihilation by the nuclear expression of military power is held in abeyance.[85] The treaty applies to the nineteen nations already possessing nuclear weapon capability. Those who did not already possess nuclear arms capability were left to shudder at the possibility that threat of nuclear war could be used as a bargaining chip to coerce supportive behavior.

Control at the international level

The United States was one of fifty states ratifying the UN treaty to control development and use of nuclear weapons, as was Russia. In February, 2019, the United States threatened to withdraw from the treaty claiming that Russia had violated its terms.[86] In its wake, the issue would leave the two countries with nuclear arms capacity free to escalate a potentially dangerous environment with threat of annihilating large parts of the planet's surface.

---

[85] See, https://www.un.org/disarmament/wmd/nuclear/npt/

[86] "U.S. Suspends Nuclear Arms Control Treaty With Russia." New York Times, Feb 1, 2019. Article found at https://www.nytimes.com/2019/02/01/us/politics/trump-inf-nuclear-treaty.html

The U.S. President at the time claimed the United States, in response to a claim of Russian violations of building missiles in Europe, was ready "to embrace a new missile defense strategy." How far back in the discussion must one recede to find cause for a new strategy? While the United States can claim support to NATO with expressed protection of Europe against nuclear threat, Russia to the extent it might be in violation of the UN Treaty claims a defense posture against potential threats from its European neighbors - specifically NATO members. That includes also the United States.

A different but similar conflict is under way over a semi-moribund treaty signed between Iran and U.S.-led Western powers applying sanctions against the Middle East country in exchange for removing nuclear arms development potential of that country. As the United States withdrew from this agreement it claimed violation by the other side. In this dispute a different profile of states, vis a vis, nuclear arms agreement violation, is exposed. Iran has voiced concern that its Middle East neighbor, Israel, is not a signatory on the UN Treaty and has been free to develop and threaten nuclear arms power.[87] That would leave Iran defenseless against its neighboring enemy.

A further profile exists in which two neighboring states with existing nuclear arms power find themselves in constant mutual threat over the disputed territory of Kashmir.[88] Both India and Pakistan claim possession of nuclear arms. The threat is open, and international players must intervene to stave off nuclear arms expression.

---

[87] "Iran threatens to withdraw from the nuclear weapons treaty." The Guardian, Article found at https://www.theguardian.com/world/2018/apr/24/iran-threatens-to-withdraw-from-nuclear-weapons-treaty-npt

[88] Discussed at https://www.dailysabah.com/op-ed/2019/09/23/the-kashmir-conflict-under-nuclear-threat

The issue here mirrors concerns about nuclear power between many other pairs of entities. Each state is concerned for its ability to defend itself against threat of nuclear war. The paradoxical solution to assuage the fear is to escalate nuclear development, by any means.

A civic engagement

Virtually half the population of the western world is exposed at one time or other to advice proudly adorning the uniform, if not the minds, of Boy Scouts. Be prepared is their group motto. It means, in this person's thinking, handle each eventuality as it arises; Don't ignore it by leaving it for someone else, or by just running away from it for lack of will.

We learn through commercial media how civil police authorities are increasing their ability to face and overcome civil unrest. A few years back, the news carried stories of how the City of Chicago had installed street cameras throughout the city to monitor citizen movement.[89] More recently, news of increasingly sophisticated technologies have been introduced to the New York City police department to combat civil unrest, that is to say, civil disobedience. Difference in this application is that New York city government officials were not informed of the placement of new surveillance technologies.[90] No doubt such enhancements occur widely across this and other countries claiming to provide better police protection for citizen safety.

---

[89] Discussed at https://www.nytimes.com/2004/09/21/us/chicago-moving-to-smart-surveillance-cameras.html

[90] See, https://www.brennancenter.org/our-work/research-reports/new-york-city-police-department-surveillance-technology

All this comes from an anti-terrorism motif re-emphasized in 2001 by the U.S. Patriot Act,91 and amended through three successive administrations with more advanced technologies and surveillance authorizations. The mind set of fear among the populace is thus established.

Ostensibly, people in the streets are safer, from domestic violence and from foreign intrusion, by virtue of enhanced militaristic police protection and policing practices. To many, this leaves a good feeling that government has taken realistic steps to assure safety and protection for its citizens, by whomever is chosen to represent them.

By stepping back from this "alarming rearming" one can gain a different perspective. Arming and rearming a civic police force may be necessary. One cannot dispute that occasional disruption in society requires vigilant attention to law enforcement.

Anywhere democratic government exists in the world one can find a need for citizens, acting out their necessary grievance against an unresponsive representative government, to voice discontent through forms of demonstration. When violence accompanies such demonstration, police response becomes necessary. Our police forces should "be prepared."

Those sitting on the law and order side of the issue claim that anticipation is a necessary element in assuring citizen safety and protection. When the objective of legislation becomes enhancement of capability for its own sake – and it doesn't hurt the industry supporting police work, one should wonder why we live in such a spiraling civic environment of escalating fear, distrust and unrest.

---

91 Discussed at https://www.justice.gov/archive/ll/highlights.htm

Government imposes measures some of its citizens (occasionally a majority) object to, and police measures are taken to address expressions of disagreement. This then requires ramping up police tactics against the demonstrators. In other words, contestable conditions are set, then measures to enforce these conditions are enacted in an effort to assure the expression of civil disobedience is controlled in such a way that theoretic violence doesn't result. It's OK for violence to be perpetrated by one side, since it has legal support, but not by the other side as individuals who disagree with how democracy is implemented against its wellbeing.

How much of the energy devoted to enhancing policing power could be invested in assuring a better democracy? Civil disobedience occurs because a significant plurality disagrees with government behavior. Some elements of society ride the coat-tails of such expression, often leading to violence. Hence the need to increase police protection may be a required response.

Too often, violence replaces the initial motivation for expressions of civil disobedience. Which gets more attention in commercial media? Is the cause of citizen push back, the push back itself, or the means to repress the push back the news item with greatest reader appeal? One should ask. If commercial media presentation is where general citizen attention is directed, the original claim against how democracy is to be practiced is all but set aside.

Is there a better, certainly less expensive, option than increasing police power? Would it be reasonable to expect a government to be just as responsive to initial claims of those demonstrating against militaristic build-up as it is in being better prepared to resist unauthorized behavior?

We need protection by police responding to legal requirements for civic behavior. We also need a democracy responsive to citizen expressions of discontent, that is to say, desire for freedom. There is overlap, and that's where the spiraling effect can be seen. One can ask why there is a spiraling effect by considering who is to gain.

Does government get to do what it wants and to protect this right by escalating powers of enforcement? Who controls such government if not the financial backing of those who gain the most by increasing the preparedness of police forces? When did democracy change its focus from improving service to citizens to improving gains of an industrial elite?92

Look to the commercial media to respond best to these questions, that is, to respond best according to the interests of its owners and financial sponsors. If we claim that an independent media might have been able to set the proper balance between police protection and civil expressions of disapproval, well, commercial media has taken care of this, too, legislatively in the U.S. No longer does independent media have access to national radio or press because distribution of news, legally, is controlled by corporations who own the means for allowing it to happen.

It's one thing to be prepared; It's another to be accountable for the elements of democracy one is prepared against. In a balanced democracy, both are supported.

At the root

Everyone seems to want the position of "king of the hill." It's a position more easily defended than having to face an up-hill climb. Every State seeks such position, or assurance that the current king will not threaten livelihood of other players. Building a strong police force is a hedge against civic

---

92 Criticism of commercial media appears in Robert Chesney's Corporate Media and the Threat to Democracy, Seven Stories Press, New York, 1997.

threat. But neither of the two postures has an answer to the resentful build-up of resistance.

Resentment against excessive police presence may come from past experiences of repression, or it could represent an inherent trait of humanity. People seem to want to be left alone to do what they choose, even if what they want is threatened by another entity already there and armed with defense.

A simple truth

Nuclear disarmament exists as an example of creating longevity for those who control the means of power. It is just as wrong to seek assurance that bad things are not developed as in using bad things to gain that assurance. Where is the debate between enough power and too much power?

Is it up to the Public Sphere to make this determination? If so, there should be a channel between the Public Sphere through elected representatives to assure policy makers decide wisely in favor of peace and not in favor of those controlling how government decides how much power is needed to be safe and secure. In a democracy, the voice of the people is collectively imperative. How this voice is stated and supported depends on the nature of discussion that seeks new ideas and evaluates them publicly.

Dialogue 12. Homo Sacer

It should not be surprising that social status, or caste, is found in virtually all societies. Each person seems to need differentiation from others on the basis of social standing. Dependent relationships develop balance against what it does not possess in order to prevent being oppressed. Difference is seen as potential conflict - a dependency unwanted and not understood. It comes when one believes in the idea of individualization, the claim that the self is the center of the universe, as the most important element to be safeguarded. This sacred position comes with threat against its existence.

In some cases, status created by difference reduces the self perceived image of the individual with lesser status, either to subjugate that individual or merely to marginalize the individual as unwanted by an elite. Those reduced in status become open targets for assaults by members of the elite. With lesser status comes further denigration, or as in Roman times to be murdered without recrimination under the law. We must be wary of laws created by the elite for the benefit of the elite.

The hood as a signal

As a society, we are asked to understand what happened in the killing of Trayvon Martin, a Florida teenager suffering under the caste of subjugation. Probably few absorbed the fundamental elements in the event.[93] By virtue of a vapid media we were exposed to what constituted a public debate over what happened, and why. The questions are easy enough. Was Martin killed

---

[93] See, "Trevor Martin shooting fast facts." CNN Library, February 28, 2019. Article found at https://edition.cnn.com/2013/06/05/us/trayvon-martin-shooting-fast-facts/index.html

because he threatened another person's life? Was the man who ended Martin's life threatened, and if so, justified in the killing? And a step back from this is the appropriateness of law in "Stand Your Ground" policies.94

Perhaps we could begin trying to understand what happened by giving George Zimmerman, the man accused of killing Martin, some legitimacy based on what he claimed to believe, or was likely to have believed.

His is a belief not uncommon across this and other nations which hold contempt for an inferior race. To believers, any step to impose acts of equality on members of a lesser social group should be considered a blemish on a higher, naturally endowed, super level of society.

Zimmerman carried an implicit obligation to establish what to him and his cohorts is consider natural order, one ordained by religious sovereignty. Sacrificing the life of someone who's very presence was anathema to what should exist comes as an obligation in order to sanctify a basic life set apart.

The same zeal was found in Europe prior to World War II, and evidently still is in the early decades of the twenty-first century, in the rebirth of Nazism.95 Only the spiritual attitude was not, never was, and still is not, confined to Nazi practices. It certainly isn't confined to Europe nor to the United States.

What is the relationship between one who embraces this belief and his/her sovereign? Someone who accomplishes work as dictated by beliefs in the purpose of the sovereign is assured a favored place in the after-life. End-

---

94 Discussed at, https://criminal.findlaw.com/criminal-law-basics/stand-your-ground-laws.html

95 See, https://www.theguardian.com/commentisfree/2018/apr/18/family-nazi-past-ideology-europe-germany-fascism-far-right

ing the life of a person of lower caste becomes an enabler to glorification. It is a fast track move to a better place.

But what are the circumstances justifying Martin's death to those who don't accept such belief? Was Martin's life merely a sacrifice, or was he, in the natural state of being who he was, hastened to that better place?

Not only are these thoughts not commonly discussed in the public domain, they are not found among those who followed the event and its trappings through the media. To subscribers of media information there is only a matter of civil law. This takes the issue back to the easy questions posed earlier about treatment of caste.

Trying to understand human behavior and what beliefs cause it to perform its various functions is not child's play. Media prevents us from thinking. It influences us to pick and choose logical support to what we already knew based only on what we read. The problem society addresses is that not everyone knows the same thing, reading as they do from different sources. That's the purpose of law. It removes loose ends in favor of a composite majority opinion, mostly the opinion of those who create law, that is, the elite.

Never mind that media helps create this opinion. We see such laws as "Stand Your Ground" because a majority views it as appropriate. How else could the subjugated be removed from the conscience of society?

The law says that Zimmerman is innocent, since it was convinced that the killing of Martin was an act of self-protection. That takes away the issue of purpose, and expectation from a higher sovereignty. It places the issue in a controllable, and even understandable, context. It remains a matter of law.

So it is

According to Roman law, a person banned from society may be killed by anyone, although the banned individual could not be sacrificed through practice of religious persecution.96 What was treated by Christian ethic that regarded the individual as sacred, was not always the application of homo sacer. Those set apart from society during the earlier period had the anticipation of divine treatment by the gods in the after-life.

It seems too convenient that in this modern period those abiding by unwritten laws that ostracize an individual by any characteristic of difference from the elite set should be free to mistreat those condemned by circumstance, as if their justifying reason would be that the gods would provide salvation to the condemned, to the extent it exists.

A simple truth

Justice should not be determined solely by statutory law, unless law reflects human values found in the individual. How can society appreciate justice without discussing it, its purpose and circumstance of its application. Can such discussion be complete without arriving at a common point of acceptance for what is believed and what should be believed about individual difference?

One major problem resulting from democratic practice is that everyone by principle tends to be treated as equal, possessing the same rights to do the same things. Individualization claims differently. In public discussion we find difference of opinion being expressed. Isn't it possible that such difference could survive efforts to align it with the democratic sameness? Isn't the

---

96 Discussed at, https://bmcr.brynmawr.edu/2010/2010.05.12/

issue worthy of discussion? With so many notions of what constitutes justice, evaluation by those concerned could result reasonably in better understanding of both need and intent for policy developers.

Part II: On governing - Controlling behavior based on what is believed

The act of governing, or governance, is a process of control either by right of authority or resulting from direct suppression of rules by behaviors of leaders. In the general notion of democracy, control occurs through acts of citizen participation. That is, government reacts to expressed wishes of participating citizens, or citizens resist to government behavior. Direct authoritarian suppression can occur through totalitarian dictatorship or through rights of succession that limit leadership to family groups or to an elite clan.

For governing by citizen granted authority, a process of law exists to define what is acceptable behavior in order to assure favorable treatment of society by the governing organ. Law also addresses behavior of citizens against themselves.

In accommodating the assertion of Thomas Hobbes that under natural law citizens are inclined to behave "brutishly," and to avoid the Machiavellian notion that the governing leader should acquire, even if through suppression, enough power to resist the tendency of citizens to revolt, behavioral laws should carry the perception that they were created with the benefit of citizens in mind, even if citizens had to be cajoled to accept them. Critical to the legitimacy of such process, and as suggested in his Letter to Richard Price, the American Thomas Jefferson insisted success of democracy depended on a "well-informed electorate."[97] Central to the meaning of this phrase is active and meaningful contribution from the Public Sphere.

Jefferson was not the only political thinker who claimed need for a well-informed electorate. Various political leaders advised against uneducated voters who would otherwise lead the country back to the tyranny it was attempting to avoid. After the Constitution had been ratified, Virginia gover-

---

[97] op. cit.

nor, William H. Cabell, asserted that education "constitutes one of the great pillars on which the civil liberties of a nation depend."98

Even before the creation of a democratic United States, education was promoted as a fundamental deontology. The practice or experience has value in and of itself. When applied to government, especially in a democracy, it occupies a fundamental role. Many of the early political leaders in the United States expounded on the importance of education for the citizens in a democracy. In "Thoughts on Government," John Adams explains the importance of education in supporting a responsive government as well as for its inherent value.99

---

98 Discussed at, https://jackmillercenter.org/virtue-educated-voter/

99 See, https://www.nps.gov/inde/upload/Thoughts-on-Government-John-Adams-2.pdf

Dialogue 13. Government is more than administration

In many parts of the world, administration refers to a managerial element overseeing governmental care for citizens. In other parts, administration focuses on specific organs of government responsible for how care of citizens is to be executed. In a democracy, where administrators of government result from citizen participation, or by elected representatives on behalf of citizens, one can see that citizens could be held responsible for governing themselves, directly or indirectly.

The Confusion

We often confuse in discussions conceptual difference between government and administration of government, and even with the democracy itself that conceptually provides a moral framework for government. Although a citizen might claim a specific meaning for or application of democracy, another citizen could reflect a different perspective, one that focuses more on specific value for preservation of self. The confusion found in discussions and then in debate is experienced when one perception seeks to impose its views on another person who claims different understanding.

Consider that governing could control individual freedoms, such as preventing citizen behavior without proper legal license. Governing also could frame freedoms through statute resulting from edict or more positively from a legislative body accepting the obligation of stewardship for total society.

Governing can also exist through the executive's acceptance of individual morality stemming either from natural or religious law; or it could result from self-proclaimed divine right. Within the vague construction of many State constitutions, any one of these meanings can be derived.

Context

A question once posted on social media called attention to a lack of clarity in what constitutes government, at least democratic government. The question appearing from the Electronic Governance (EGOV) Community Group asks, "Is government turning from a Service Provider to an information clearinghouse?"100 This question is interesting as it suggests a growing role for government to distribute information beyond formal structuring for how citizen needs are to be supported.

Those with an opinion on the matter tend to share, through the many blog sites set up to address the topic, thoughts on whether information sharing is or is not a critical element for government. Is it the business of government to become an information clearing house? If so, in what manner is the information to be developed to serve both the functions of governance and to inform the public?

Two related issues can be found at the heart of the question. One deals with what constitutes the structure of government, and the second deals with how different elements within this structure address performance of government services. The interaction between them serves a purpose for coordination of information content. Big Data as a structural concept for managing information is the precipitous element calling attention to how government information services are supported.

---

[100] Activities of the Group are found at, https://www.w3.org/community/egovernance/

Issue 1: With respect to functions of government. Assuming we limit perspective to constitutional democracies, government consists of two major sub-organizations. One deals with law-making, and the other deals with administering or enforcing the law. If reference to informational needs which satisfy citizen services really addresses only the administrative body of government - the latter administrative sub-organization, we deal only partly with government through its internal requirements for information. Need for information by citizens, the first sub-organization, is not addressed, other than to consider how specific law relates to information collection and dissemination is authorized and developed.

Conversations, such as posted in community blogs, typically reflect casual references to government and too often miss the constitutional relationship between two distinctly different functional bodies. In doing so they do not acknowledge a dominant and supportive linkage between them.

Legislation and administration do not often seem interdependent, but their connecting processes require access to the same information and treat it as a common pool of information for governance. Relevance for intellectual contribution to these conversations is limited because the two roles perform distinctly different duties. One role addresses legislative need for the information; the other addresses how it is to be used to satisfy that need. A society behaving under the rule of law that grants access might suffer limitations in public discourse that ignores legal time stamps for collection of aging data, constraining contemporary relevance.

Issue 2: With respect to public need for accessing collected information. As part of an administrative function of government, and as dictated by the legislative function, government is obliged to provide informational services specifically in response to citizen demands. Is administrative government obliged to provide informational services in response to broader legislative demands as part of a constitutional relationship and only consequentially in support of citizen needs or to citizen demands? Is information focused on support to citizens? Or, does it focus on an effective infrastructure serving administrative requirements of governance?

Administrative officials, those of the Bureaucracy, are trapped in the process. Constitutional requirements call for them to respond directly to legislative regulatory commitments which they assist in developing through a budgetary process. At the same time, they deal as direct points of contact with citizens and feel sympathy to help resolve problems local to their respective communities (health care, transportation, justice, other). The three-way Iron Triangle behavior described by Hugh Heclo pits policy influential forces in the Bureaucracy with legislative processes in congressional committees and actions of special interest represented by regulated groups outside the constitutional framework for government.101

The bottom line is that in speaking about governments as if they were administrative entities only, we should bear in mind that we deal incompletely in satisfying citizen service needs for information. Requirements for information collection, retention, and dissemination are determined by a legislative body of government with no direct responsibility singularly to support citizen needs.

Separation of Functional Power

Constitutionally overlapping powers and iron triangle relationships suggest that both legislative and administrative elements of government should work together in a government highly dependent on information develop-

---

101 Heclo, Hugh, A Government of Strangers: Executive Politics in Washington, Brookings Institute, 1977.

ment and sharing. An implicit benefit of separation is that neither source of power would control government and its use for information.

Alexander Hamilton presented in Federalist Paper Number 67 the idea supporting the manner decided by the Framers to elect members of their government. He presented in Federalist Paper Number 68 the need for separation of powers such that no single source of power was to reside in a single Branch of government.

While distribution of power was determined in such manner as to avoid tyranny by any element in power, a special Electoral College process was developed. This process elected the single executive by combination of voting powers of citizens and States. Citizen voices were included in their elected representatives in the House of Representatives and the members of the elected Senate characterizing voices of the individual states.

While the distribution of power within the formal structure of a democratic government had been determined constitutionally, it was not until later that a broader distribution of power could be detected in explaining how the act of governance could be understood. In addition to the two influences on information capture and distribution found in the Legislative Branch and in the Bureaucracy of the Executive Branch within a democracy, a third informal branch appeared through involvement of special interest groups. These groups influence thinking of bureaucrats and members of subcommittees in the Congress specific to informational need.

Special care was taken in determining structure and behavior of government under the Constitution to accommodate different information needs. Different perspectives were in conflict, lacking central and common justification of purpose. This formative document provided guidance for both the structure of government and the means by which governance was to be carried out. The structure would assure formal identification of information needs and the means for providing it.

A simple truth

In practice, an informal process assures consistency in how government represents information needs of different, mutually dependent, power sources: government, the collective regulated industry, and members of the public.

A recent event that might have disrupted the balance between the three influential elements for a democratic government is seen in Citizens United,102 as undue influence was adjudicated by the Supreme Court in favor of demands from extra-governmental groups. The private sector introduces its voice as influence for government action. Where does this leave power from the public if it reduces relative influence on the formation of governance and the purpose intended to support all three of Heclo's elements?

If members of the Public Sphere cannot develop a singular voice, what chance exists for focusing power arising from citizen influential participation? How might influential power from such singular voice be developed if public discussion and debate does not occur?

102

, 21 January 2010.

Dialogue 14. Other than genocide

The military component in war presents serious problems for society. Imminent death of combatants is hard to justify based on generally accepted moral principles worldwide. Yet, no nation has been under the illusion that military action could be conducted without experiencing or causing death.

A curious relationship exists between the act of war and the cause of war. Is there no case where military aggression did not follow a provocative political aggression? How much destruction of an enemy's military forces is needed to satisfy decision makers anxious to resort to killing to justify political assertion of power? Or, is there an additional motivation toward killing in battle?

Applications of killing

The International Criminal Tribunal at the Hague a few years ago found General Ratko Mladić, accused of genocide in the mass killing of Muslim males at Srebrenica, guilty of war crimes. Although not much discussion made its way at the time into commercial media, reporting appeared in other publications, notably Foreign Policy magazine. Of particular note in that publication was a running debate between reporter Michael Dobbs, who cited claims that genocide was appropriate, and bloggers who claimed that Dobbs's journalism was biased, lacking both appropriate perspective and lack of objectivity.

The issue is indeed an ugly one, as no matter which way the Criminal Tribunal could have gone, thousands of men and boys lost their lives, and thousands of other citizens were forced to leave their homes. (Not unlike any other war!)

The acrimony surrounding Dobbs's material continues to this date. One element that seems appropriate to debate is in how genocide is defined. Guilt for mass killing at Srebrenica can leave no doubt, as the Court found. But, if the accusation is genocide, the fact that only males were killed, a circumstantial condition in any war, then genocide hardly applies because females were not conscripted into combat roles in Eastern Europe countries.

One might assert that the issue of genocide (or not) makes little difference in characterizing what General Mladić was found guilty of.[103] The notion behind mass killing, as indicated by most of the evidence, might bring other war atrocities before a tribunal. How many ways might mass killing be defined? Was the atomic bombs over Hiroshima and Nagasaki under the direction of then President Harry S. Truman examples of mass killing? Was the My Lai massacre in 1968 at the direction of U.S. Army Second Lieutenant William Calley an example at a smaller scale? Could the bombing of Panama City in 1989 by U.S. forces under the direction of then President George H.W. Bush also be considered mass killing? Did any of the latter events focus uniquely on males, the active participants in war at the time?

Maybe it's the repugnant manner in which the killings at Srebrenica took place. Does manner suggest other circumstances be put aside? What about moral reasons for such killing?

We could not anticipate before the fact the outcome of the case at the Hague. Issues such as Mladić's poor health disturbed the process of justice.

---

[103] General Mladić was found guilty in 1992 on 10 of 11 war crime charges, but was not found guilty of genocide.

We can only wonder how we could incorporate justification for the cause of military action in the same vein as we incorporate applications of justice for the behavior of military action, or for result of any other violence against society.

A simple truth

Contemporary use of military action appears to follow Clausewitz thinking that such use represents failed political policy. Policy addressing different and conflicting views of human behavior addresses latent Hobbesian bestiality in humanity. Rather than attempting to rid expressions of such difference between views of Clausewitz and Hobbes, policy might more reasonably attempt to address how difference could be accommodated. But then, perhaps it is such difference that suggests a reality for humanity that includes means through brutality for challenging, if not ridding, society behavior from elements of social conflict. But should we accept that the result should favor the strong over the weak?

Dialogue 15. Tyranny as antithesis of freedom

A social contract between society and government addresses assurances of security and service in exchange for civil obedience. The application of this exchange defines how members of society understand their freedoms. When control applied to limit benefits to a society follows arbitrary or capricious indifference to societal needs, legitimacy of government is questioned. The result is uncertainty and discontent among citizens. Their collective sense of freedom is thus undermined.

Tyranny is that control over society by any form of leadership that deprives individuals of their natural freedoms. Most of us would accept that tyrannical rule - setting aside the manner by which it is attained - is imposition of power without legitimacy. While tyranny is not unique to governmental oppression, we often speak of it in that context.

Case in point

In the United States today, questionable policies developed from legislation passed by elected leadership, and political behaviors of this leadership claimed contradictory to protections and assurances written in the Constitution, bring tyranny into discussion.

Liberal politicians claim that conservative leadership nullifies what society's majority holds as constitutionally assured, essentially ignoring provisions under a Social Contract that natural freedoms should be supported. On the other side, conservative politicians basing perspectives on interpretations of original intent claim this focus of social support has become too liberal, that liberal leadership over the past two centuries has systematically perverted the Constitution's application in assuring stability.

A dispute between two Justices on the Supreme Court, where constitutional interpretation is expected to occur, makes it clear that different polarity among political ideologies exists between original intent and value in context for that intent. This was an especially popular debate in 2006 and again in 2009 between Justice Scalia who argued the conservative position focused on original intent and Justice Breyer who argued the liberal position supporting a changing society.104

Apparent in claims and behaviors of liberal leaders, conservatives believe the Constitution, as amended, could provide a basis for democracy, but applicability in law must be determined by relevant value for society. The development of constitutional amendments in the view of conservatives might suggest this departure as prima facie liberalism, supporting the claim that liberal political processes move government beyond the reach of the original Constitution.

A public debate follows between a conservative original intent and a liberal living document. Conservatives avoid discussions of tyranny regarding claims of overly strict government rulings by citing a return to historical foundations - what the Framers intended in 1791. To them, any governmental behavior contrary to original thinking of the Framers could be considered tyrannical - government thus lacking a legitimate basis. Assuring justice in the thinking of the Framers, a conservative contends, was focused on need for order, power, tradition and authority under the law.

From the perspective of liberalism, at least insofar as the Constitution is concerned, times have changed, and so have social values and needs, and

---

104 View the 2009 debate at, https://www.youtube.com/watch?v=jmv5Tz7w5pk

hence basis for support from constitutional language. A "Living Constitution" becomes the justification for constitutional assurance of justice in a contemporary context. Hence the conflict between liberalism and conservatism as practiced in America.

To a conservative, any government behavior which cannot reflect historical trappings of an amended Constitution should be rejected altogether. Witness behaviors of recent congresses successfully setting aside or negating many of the provisions of the Bill of Rights such as limiting voting rights, or following the suggestion of former House Speaker, Newt Gingrich.105 The Speaker advanced the practice of religion in government's perspective of democracy since such practice was suggested in framing documents even if contrary to language in the Establishment Clause of the Constitution.106

Tyranny has a different progenitor than contradiction to constitutional protection with its fundamental anchor to assure citizen freedoms. The loss of a truly representative government dislodges legitimacy for any society seeking to be protected by democratic principles. Rather than debating the loss of constitutional protections and assurances due to excessive liberalism, today's conservative leaders promote legislative actions that support their self-serving agenda by resisting liberal interpretation of changing social values.

---

[105] Gingrich, Newt, Winning the Future: A Twentieth Century Contract with America, Regnery Publishing, 2005.

[106] The First Amendment to the U.S. Constitution forbids Congress from establishing a State religion.

Tyranny through religion

Tyranny can result from sources other than government - viewing government in the strict sense of organized representation of social interests. Religion is a partner of equal standing with government in tyrannical practice. Tyranny over citizen rights is present in claims of control over individual behavior following religious principles. "God-given rights" are inalienable, as pronounced in U.S. Declaration of Independence. States may not deprive individuals of these rights, subject to how the nature of God is interpreted.

As a result of lost legitimacy through limited constitutional power, religious authority is more insidious. Representative government at least has rational values in which practices can be evaluated by the public along with scientific expectations for evidence. Rational values have little value for religion.

For starters, government leaders are chosen by the people over which power can be imposed, legitimately or not. Religious leaders, by and large, are self appointed, bringing with them unique claims of understanding the nature of humanity and its causes that are viewed by followers as somewhat credible in terms of what they are socialized to believe. Evidence for religion is left to vague concepts such as "faith" or "belief." That means factless expectations that something favorable will happen for them in the afterlife in spite of behavior influenced by statute reflecting rational values in legislative law.

A cognitive principle developed socially in early periods of civilization reveals how individuals bind together on issues of belief, relying on these principles for matters of behavioral control. Beliefs in source of control may be logical, as in a governmental structure of law, or it can derive from imagined sources, such as through myth or sources of supernatural power.

Once the supernatural belief element exercises its influence on an individual, the bond with a specific religion becomes unbreakable – even in the presence of controvertible evidence to the contrary, or even from rational elements of law. The insidiousness in this relationship is that participation in religious bonding loses awareness that tyranny has taken hold. No longer is the individual free to exercise independent thinking, judgment, and behavior regarding life or its exigencies. For many, this process is reasonably expected from religious doctrine. Judgment should remain with a spiritual force even for issues defined by statute.

Schism in recent practice of Democracy

A meaningful alignment of religious and governmental issues occupies the attention of Americans in today's society. Abortion, birth control, euthanasia, same-gender marriage, stem cell research are among the issues with relevance in both systems of social consideration. A "mission from God" provided impetus for military engagement in the decision of President George W. Bush to order the U.S. invasion of Iraq in 2003. Threats to individual rights, for doctors and patients, in the legal question of abortion continue to be campaign issues for both conservative candidates who want to end freedoms supported in the liberal Roe v. Wade Supreme Court ruling and liberal candidates who want to protect them. President George W. Bush ended practices of government-funded research based on human stem cells, and prohibition relaxed under liberal President Barack Obama appears to be threatened under current President Donald Trump.

While many limitations to marriage by petitioners of the same gender have lessened, some restrictions remain at the State level. Since religion lies at the base of these issues, they are paramount for determining government policy. It is therefore significant that non-religious individuals who might not have interest in expressing a position for these issues are underrepresented by America's elected conservative leaders.

Results

The question occurring to many who sense loss of freedom and who claim objectively from existence of a tyrannical relationship with government or religion is: How is a tyrannical bond dissolved? The answer lies in the nature of belief.

Government's tyrannical behavior is based on rational belief in either strict constitutional interpretation or in expectation that decisions are made in the interest of safety and well-being, with or without constitutional guidance. Religion's tyranny is based on non-rational belief imposed from sources claimed as beyond human influence.

Belief is a target for reflection. What we believe and why we believe it results primarily from socialization. Much influence on socialization is self-perpetuating, lacking opportunity for refutation. The lacked ingredient in any belief that permits tyranny to work its controlling nature is evidence gathered objectively, permitting discussion, challenge or resistance. Either we gather evidence to justify support in that which exercises power over expectation for freedom, or we submit to that which perpetuates tyranny.

A simple truth

It seems clear that society wants or needs some explanation for human behavior that does not exist rationally. Religious belief reasonably satisfies that end. But religion is relevant to the individual and not to society, since each person's need for explanation is uniquely different. This is why religious expression does not belong in government. Bias from religious belief and practice prevents the individual from examining his/her own personal values, that is, values personally derived. At the same time, common belief holds society together. Plato invites debate on such issues. Even this early thinker found value in religious belief, but he left social issues in the hands of discussants. This is where truth is discovered in support of a democratic government.

Dialogue 16. To vote or not to vote

In a democracy each citizen is offered a chance to participate in determining how government is to perform and who its leaders should be. Such participation occurs either directly by virtue of referendum voting, or in influential communication with elected officials, or it could occur indirectly through representative voting. In other words, democracy is a form of government by the people in which supreme social power is vested in the people and exercised directly by them or indirectly through their elected agents under a system of free elections.

While measurable results favoring citizen acceptance of government is found in voting, one might wonder if voters have real choices to elect individuals who might represent their interests, favorably. The process of voting is influenced by a number of factors. On the positive side, voting can follow specific political ideologies, such as conservatism, socialism, liberalism, even progressivism. Facilitation of the process may be limited by structural barriers, such as registration requirements, voting access points, transportation needs and accommodation for disabilities at voting locations. Language can also be a limiting barrier in cases of immigrating citizens and their families for which they speak.

Past voting behavior often reveals weakness in each element of the voting process that would limit how this participative element of democracy is practiced. One persistent element for determining quality of democracy appears in effectiveness in the process that produces leaders.

Cases from history

Putting aside acrimony resulting from elections in two strong democracies, we can consider national elections held in the United States and in France, each a bastion of different methods for representative democracy. In both countries the dominant rhetoric addressing the personality and character of a specific candidate is found rather than focus on issues critical to citizens. Such focus diverts real questions for democracy from real social problem issues and principles to address popularity of individual candidates, and consequently on issues in their respective election platforms.

In France, popular discourse in 2012 focused on the strategy needed by President Nicolas Sarkozy to triumph in his bid for re-election. Media reporting of his financial alignment with the wealthy and too closeness with controversial leaders in other unfriendly countries found disfavor among voters. In the United States, daily news sources focused the general population on the use of social networks as a strategy by President Barack Obama in his bid for re-election. Strategies considered important by these individuals to win their respective contests focused more on the influence of journalism than in determining specific needs of citizens. In fact, needs of citizens were rarely discussed in campaign rhetoric for each election; significantly, non-debated issues such as high unemployment, tax reduction, social welfare, personal rights, civil liberties and national defense remained under-discussed.

Shift in popular thinking for France was expressed in the media as a reactive pushback from conservative practices of the existing administration, while in the United States continuity of existing liberal practices was emphasized. Was anyone left to determine for him/herself what political ideology issues really meant for the livelihood of individual voters? Was high unemployment so basic an issue that everyone could be assumed to possess the same understanding of its relationship with liberty and freedom? Was discussion and debate of these issues not necessary? Was social welfare such a basic issue as to be ignored contrary to any voter supporting socialistic or communistic practices?

It would be relevant to consider what constitutes a more reasonable debate for or against candidate qualifications. Consider, for example, the issue of urban traffic gridlock in the United States or the issue of fair trade arrangements for French farmers or fishermen. In neither case did citizens across the broader political spectrum understand what was involved in considering a country-wide problem, much less in evaluating and accepting a proposed governmental policy that addressed individual interests - what the candidates believed was important. Yet, an electioneering candidate, through presentation by the commercial media, could claim a platform for assuring appropriate legislation to solve all ills (as undefined as they may be), just by claiming a particular political ideology, or because a popular figure in cinema or sport would express support for the candidate.

A drama of competition captures the interest of a voting public. President Sarkozy was presented in French media by the message, La France forte![107] President Obama was dramatized as the man who rescued America from oppressive overly strict avoidance of social needs by earlier administrations. Is it any wonder citizens are trapped in support of the claim of emotionally and sensationally baited entertaining elements found in national elections?

Is it not fair to claim that as part of voting behavior citizens want to be entertained, to be distracted from problematic issues of daily living? Or, is it

---

[107] A strong France

that citizens want an elected leader who would through some chimeric magic lead them to better living? In either case, can anyone see a role for representative government in a manner different from electing Miss America or Miss France, or can assure a world championship in a sport of one's choosing? I suppose what we want as voters is freedom of choice (sounds like something constitutional) in how we will be entertained and perhaps what we will be entertained by.

Issue around the Electoral College

In a nutshell, the electoral college is an indirect or intermediate level process for voting. A constitution characterizes the method as a compromise between election of government officials by citizens and representation of geopolitical regions in which the country is divided. The process is used in the United States to elect the president. In France it is used to elect members of le Senate. The original idea behind the process was to avoid duplicating voting power of citizens and of jurisdictions of the country as subordinate elements of a collective whole.

Those who argue against the process claim it takes power away from citizen voters, and is thereby undemocratic. Advocates of the process claim it avoids putting unbalanced voting power in favor of more heavily populated regions, and additionally they advance the notion that putting all the power in citizens risks putting officials in office based on opinions of uneducated voters who lack awareness of both candidate qualifications and needs of the general population.

Democracy pundits claim that every vote counts, and they push for more active practice of voting rights. Constitutional framers warned against unfair influence from factions of these voters, specifically formed as political parties. We might note this advisory of James Madison in "Federalist No. 10" of the Federalist Papers.

Lacking traction after several legislative attempts to abolish the Electoral College in the United States, detractors focus on tangential issues such as gerrymandering at the fringes of what constitutes democracy through election of the president. Better effects for improving democracy through voting would result by reducing influence of political parties and corporate sponsors on elections and on the legislative process. However, if the focus is to remain on power to the people, one might consider a bit of American history.

First thought is to retain influence of geopolitical regions (states in the United States) against influence of citizens. The idea of the Framers was to create balance between the two entities: states through the Senate and citizens through the House of Representatives. Together, their collectively balanced influence was translated through voting in the Electoral College. Unfortunately for this balancing, the 17th Amendment to the U.S. Constitution took power away from state legislatures in determining senators and placed it in the hands of citizen voters within respective states. This action destroyed the balance in voting between state legislatures and citizens originally intended. Today, those who claim the president and vice president together should be elected directly by citizens, contrary to provisions of the greatly neutered Electoral College, put all the power in the hands of voting citizens.

So should it be, if balance of power between states and citizens no longer has purpose, that all power should reside with citizens. However, this presents an even larger issue requiring deeper consideration than any tangential issue such as gerrymandering. That issue occurs in the dependability of informed voting. Why should all the power in electing government officials fall in the hands of elements so easily influenced by bias in the media or from voices in the entertainment industry - to which one might add sports? Specific to the 2016 presidential election, why should voters have been restricted to two very polarizing candidates determined by political party dynamics rather than through potential support to democratic principles?

If practice of democracy follows the very liberal views of Jean-Jacques Rousseau and allows citizens to elect whom they believe appropriate based on service to democracy, at least society could think about reducing the effect on democracy from those elected based on social popularity, specifically appropriate in the case of electing the president.

A simple truth

Perhaps in a world tending to respond to social preferences for electing a president, elected legislators could follow through check and balance power provisions according to what was intended by the Framers as the more important body and hold the president in check. Rather than focusing on the process for electing officials, more attention could be paid to a means to assure that an official once elected would uphold the requirements of the office.

The theory behind the electoral college might be challenged, but is election based on political party pressure a better means for electing officials in a democracy? The democratic movement in the United States has moved far beyond what was intended in the Constitution. If such movement is supportable, a new constitution is required, rather than one with pasted amendments aimed toward changing or clarifying original intent.

Such discussion of voting power, to the extent it occurs, could gain more weight when it includes officials elected to represent the voters, rather than party allegiance or their own personal interests. Citizens could base voting decisions on what they believe rather than on what another political entity influences them to believe.

Dialogue 17. Rule of law - for whom?

In a democracy, is the law king? The Center for Constitution Rights reports a long history of U.S. war-making and conflict related human rights violations throughout its history in spite of law, at least constitutional law, and not specifically related to its war on terror, declared in 2001 following the "9/11" attacks in New York city and at the Pentagon.

U.S. military treatment of detainees at locations in Afghanistan, Guantánamo Bay, Iraq, and at secret "black site" locations around the world following the 9/11 attacks has undermined international law in disregard to fundamental human rights, according to the Center for Constitutional Rights.108 The U.S. claimed, in its defense, that such treatment was not covered under international law citing national defense as a justification. Nevertheless, others claim the government's prisoner interrogation techniques, solitary confinement procedures, and its failure to provide "full and fair" trials at detention centers, violate provisions in the Geneva Conventions and basic human rights.

At an international war crimes tribunal in Malaysia, specific to claims of prisoner maltreatment, the U.S. President, Vice President and other U.S. government officials were found guilty of war crimes, crimes against humanity and other like offenses as recognized under International Law.109 As to the legitimacy of the court, it lacks legal binding for its findings and

---

[108] Discussion found at, https://ccrjustice.org/home/get-involved/events/join-ccr-president-michael-ratner-discussion-uss-continued-violations

[109] The Kuala Lumpur War Crimes Tribunal found U.S. President George W Bush and British Prime Minister Tony Blair guilty in 2011 of crimes against peace, crimes against humanity, and genocide as a result of their roles in the Iraq War.

cannot enforce them. Nevertheless, it is claimed that a U.S. legal entity supported the legal process.

The prosecution team for the tribunal was mentored by Richard Baxter of
the Harvard Law School. Baxter was the person primarily responsible for
preparing the 1956 edition of U.S. Army Field Manual 27-10 regarding the
law of land warfare. He had also served as Chief of the International Law
Branch, Office of the Judge Advocate General, for the U.S. military.

No doubt, White House staffs (earlier and present) were aware of
actions and persons involved. Too much power is located in these named
sources to think hopefully that the Malaysia proceedings resulted in something material to the gravity of the charges. Should the U.S. President be
concerned? Is a U.S. president not above the law? Neither Presidents Andrew Jackson nor Richard Nixon claimed otherwise, publicly.

The issue of executive privilege goes further in favor of claims in support
of extra-legal presidential behavior with respect to legislated law. Under the
protection of confidentiality, communication between the president and
aides, especially where defense and national security are concerned, are protected. President Nixon's lawyers argued in the "Watergate Case" that "absolute executive privilege was based only on his discretion."110 The behavior
of the current U.S. President, Donald Trump, demonstrates publicly the
same perspective. In his case, due to sympathetic political ideological
alignment the Supreme Court may absent itself from determining the answer.

One might think that war crimes and related behavior considered by
law or moral imperative should result in some sort of punishment, perhaps

---

110 Discussed at, https://www.landmarkcases.org/united-states-v-nixon/us-v-nixon-back-
ground-summary-3

even very harsh punishment fitting the crime. Shouldn't one expect that even before launching the invasion of Iraq in 2003, the Bush Administration had already initiated efforts to assure it couldn't be held accountable even though customary international law holds such purported grants of immunity void ab initio, from the outset?

Maybe the question should be, are America's elected officials through "right of passage" exempt from judicial proceedings of other nations for criminal acts committed against their respective sovereignties or against their citizens according to an applicable international legal code? Even if the answer is in the affirmative, how long would it take the U.S. to withdraw financial support from linking international entities, like United Nations, UNICEF, International Red Cross, and many others which provide support to beleaguered citizens, resulting from un-controlled political entities?

Can anyone imagine the Hague issuing a warrant to arrest a senior U.S. official found to have committed a crime? The United States has long contended that actions by the International Criminal Court have no standing in the United States for lack of ratification.111

Does a crime committed in a different political jurisdiction count as a crime if the perpetrators can get away with it? Would history books record it as a crime? Does law work only when it serves the purpose of those who create it, or of those who can dismiss it as irrelevant? Does a universal value system, morally speaking, exist anywhere other than in the thinking of Immanuel Kant? Kant would claim that universal moral law exists only to the extent it is accepted by everyone, a phenomenon restricted to nature. Do elected officials "check their morals at the door" upon taking office? If international agreements had any weight whatsoever, the United States, Great

---

[111] Discussed at, https://scholarlycommons.law.wlu.edu/wlufac/504/

Britain and their allies might never have been in the Middle East following the 2003 invasion, and President Bush, et al., would never have been tried in absentia as a result of war crimes demonstrated to have been committed.

As a society, we tend to dismiss accountability for leaders whose judgment goes astray of conventional morality. We expect these larger forces to take care of business. When the result of business is otherwise than expected, who is accountable for the failure? Who even gets to declare the failure? Whom do we hold responsible for violating rules laid before society? How can we expect to hold responsible, based on violated rules, those who developed the rules in the first place? Is the rule pre-eminent, or is the rule-maker above the law?

Perhaps expecting accountability cannot be done, as claimed by those who study sovereignty. Machiavelli claimed the rule-maker must be above the rule of law. If one is to believe that states draw motivation from their own instinct to survive and prosper, and that true international authority is unachievable, then one would be hard-pressed to admit that any rule-maker should abide by a rule that truly punished him/her or restricted their behavior. We need only look to the veto power of the permanent members of the UN Security Council to see how realist self-interest trumps liberal idealism.

We live in a time when such question is before us, to respond in deed, or to abide by its subconscious anchor. Every society (sans donnée présise112) exists in a mode of wanting, needing someone, some entity to take responsibility for all that society does, for all its experiences, for its failures (even to define what is a failure), and for all its guidance. We know nothing about

---

112 Without precise data

need for this surreal entity, but nevertheless we create religion to rationalize it. Then we create a reality to transform such leadership into a societal role.

Presidents have been exalted and reviled; and societal response has had little disturbing effect on the office. But the role seems to have evolved beyond the political (which is to say government politic) and taken on a personal, even spiritual dimension. On what other basis could U.S. voters have elected their three most recent presidents?

As citizens we turn to the "rule of law" to express our displeasure in contemporary presidential behavior. On any previous occasion of displeasure, we would have based it on moral grounds, citing what the individual believed or what was represented to be outside (not above) the law. We've turned around the relationship with presidents. Now we elect on spiritual grounds (as society's savior) and criticize based on law. Yet, there have been exceptions, such as Andrew Jackson, Richard Nixon, and Donald Trump.

So, we arrive at a question: In a democracy, do we really want, can we really trust, another member of society to represent our non-rational spiritual needs, which is to suggest behavior outside rational law, or do we elect from among the masses and hold the individual accountable for conformance to legislated or judicial law?

A simple truth

Laws are created by those with power to do so. If their purpose is to protect the givers of law, and not to be used against them, what then becomes of the adage that in a presidential democracy any person can become president? Why should any elected president be expected to attain glorification at the hands of voters? We might claim that leadership in a democracy is determined by the choice of citizens. Is this realistic, that is, is it appropriate that this choice has no rational, objective basis? Other than through common perspective, arrived at through an active Public Sphere, how can such base for voting decisions be understood?

Dialogue 18. Is Democracy Oedipal

According to the tale from Sophocles, Oedipus is prophesied in the Oracle of Delphi to murder his father and marry his mother. From this tale the psychoanalysts, notably Sigmund Freud, claim that a fundamental behavior exists in all males such that they possess a love desire for the mother.

In conventional relationships for democracy, the state is treated as the mother of society, as it possesses the responsibility to protect and serve its members. Freud makes no distinction between a son-mother and daughter-father relationship following the tale, but society's choice for democracy provides the separation - from which the female rebels.

Society of the male seeking care; government as the caring mother

Is democracy an appropriate form of government, considering the needs of society's demand for constant caring? Is democracy to be applauded because it is based on a constitution and citizens vote, or is there something psychoanalytic to suggest a relationship other than constitutional? Should the child be expected to care for itself, or at least to influence its care through a sense of expressed individual need?

From the Preamble to the U.S. Constitution in 1789 we find, "We the people of the United States, in order to form a more perfect union, establish justice, insure domestic tranquility, provide for the common defense, promote the general welfare, and secure the blessings of liberty to ourselves and our posterity, do ordain and establish this Constitution for the United States of America."113 Assuming democracy evolves appropriately from the precepts of a valid constitution, what should inform such constitution?

With a focus on "more perfect union" there is an implication that progress occurs to increase the measure of perfection. Webster-Merriam provides as useful a definition of perfection as any other dictionary.114 Apart from its characterization of a fixed and existing state of flawlessness, it allows for a progressive movement toward maturity or toward attaining a desired state in the ideal.

Amendments seem a reasonable means to accomplish this objective of positive movement, but considering the twenty-seven successful amendments of the thirty-three submitted to states for ratification and more than one hundred submissions still in abeyance, how many serve the purpose of progressive improvement? The first ten served as detail for defining rights and liberties, and only five others address issues related to items in the Preamble - issues of freedom (absence of governmental imposed restrictions against the Declaration's assurance that "all men are created equal").

While without too much tongue in cheek it can be claimed that democracy supports the best form of government. Where is it found that the best is good enough?

Resolution of the trouble points in American history during which serious problems challenged constitutional intent, it was not the democratic process that came to the aid of society. It was leadership. (The fact that leaders have been brought into positions of power does not demonstrate dependence on

---

113 Found at, https://www.law.cornell.edu/constitution/preamble

114 Being entirely without fault or defect; corresponding to an ideal standard or abstract concept

scientific analysis.) If progressive improvement could depend on "an informed populace" to determine the best candidates for leadership, democracy could have a chance to aid society through government. Since from the very first period of American history it was warned that the general public was incapable of serving such need, and since then has indelibly demonstrated that it can't, why claim such idealistic prospect for the future?

Democracy as mother

Any method providing a means, if not assurance, for quality leadership would result from a democratic method if the leadership provided the level of care expected from the mother. One might anticipate that in a mother role, the female might perform better than the male. Yet, males have dominated serving government's leadership requirement. But, what principles of leadership exist uniquely in the male? Could a female assuming a male role just as well provide leadership skills for caring for citizens?

Those who understand the oedipal relationship between those in power - those seeking it, those serving its production, and subordinates to that power - see where citizens fit in the scheme of democracy. If the child is to be cared for, following guidance from John Locke, can it be supported that citizens bear the responsibility for choosing the mother? Perhaps there is a difference between government as the female and perspectives of males who occupy leadership positions.

A simple truth

The general population in any society, democratic or not, behaves as parentless children. They are responsible for determining their well being by behavior, or in a democracy by being asked to vote. Some may claim that voters have the experience of understanding previous elected leaders, but there is no defined trend toward such ideal upon which democracy is assumed. Where is the evolution of mature understanding of the relationship between citizens and mother government to be found? Is the Public Sphere so wanting for lack of discourse as to miss the need for understanding difference between governing and mothering?

Dialogue 19. Whither goest enforcement for law and order

There is a theory that those in positions of power seek to dominate society in order to preserve their self-possessed sense of what is right or what they think should be. Social dominance theory, according to Sidanius and Pratto, is particularly dangerous in a democracy in which each citizen is considered equal in terms of social justice.115 A set of guiding social principles based on one or more of three basic elements (age, gender, ethnicity) lead to group behaviors that often rise above the rule of law. Any time these principles, singularly but more pronounced together, influence human social grouping resulting from surplus economic values, behaviors tend to reflect guiding strength from the grouping rather than from legislative elements in a democracy.

In recent rhetoric from the White House, the President claimed that with respect to lack of effective policy to control immigration, the government should "… immediately, with no Judges or Court Cases, bring (sic) them back from where they came. Our system is a mockery to good immigration policy and Law and Order."116 In ignorance of protections from legislation based on the Fourteenth Amendment of the U.S. Constitution, the President's claim suggests that those who already enjoy privilege of citizenship should be protected from all others.

―――――――――――

[115] Access to Social Dominance: "An Intergroup Theory of Social Hierarchy and Oppression" can be found at, https://www.cambridge.org/core/books/social-dominance/ ADA29C256881001463D6E2777404DB95

[116] Donald J. Trump Twitter on June 24 2018.

Social dominance resulting from existential characteristics in society form the basis for social acceptance of behavior differing from any of its elements. In the case of immigration, common ethnicity becomes the measure of legality. This does not address the contentious issue behind how law and order for those in government executive positions is based disproportionately on "order" above "law." Social dominance provides its own order.

In practice

The mind is no longer shocked by tales of abusive law enforcement or of societal members disrespectful toward acceptable rules of behavior drawn from law to provide the best safety for the public, at large. Each of us might be among an enormously large component of public service advocates who support any effort undertaken to find a better means of assuring safety for both the public and for those commissioned to serve it, but at the same time to provide the liberty claimed to reside inherently in democracy.

Success in policing appears virtually unattainable. Based on much literature about the issue, expectations for application of law and order far exceed either administration or certainly intent. What makes the issue of law enforcement so difficult is that expectations are not held in common between the government which sets them, the agencies who enforce them and the society served. Neither is the performance of those tasked to accomplish vaguely described duties at levels acceptable due to flexible evaluations.

Somewhere in the broad continuum of expectation for law and order, following need and performance based on ability, there must be a starting point from which any law enforcement discipline can be defined along with support accountable for administering it. Such a point could not be defined without compromising need and condemning those who are tasked to be responsible for satisfying its legal objectives.

At the base of any need for social control can be found an inherent condition of man, reflected in Thomas Aquinas's 13th century religious philosophy, Machiavelli's 16th century political philosophy, and more recently explained in the 17th century liberal philosophy of Thomas Hobbes. According to these philosophers, humans are born as sinners or as brutal creatures burdened with uncontrollable self-interest. In forms of societies one must deal with a means to accommodate inherent tendencies to do harm to self and others while accommodating an individualism that seeks what Greek philosophers referred to pleonexia, man's innate desire to accumulate more in order to develop potential to grow and to advance.

On the law and order side of the continuum are definable and accountable forms of control. A society which boasts serving freedoms toward liberty for the individual must assure that cost of conformity does not exceed a level of financial accommodation and not be at variance with what is believed by a minority (those opposing the demands of a majority) for support to strict regulatory behavior in assuring public safety. Otherwise, tyranny by the majority exists.

The task for such assurance is insurmountable, as demonstrated by centuries of behavior at all levels of law and order efforts. In order to be effective, any attempt to improve the condition of need for law enforcement must focus on strict definitions of intent. Such intent results from compromise by legislators who attempt to balance cost and effect ratios determined both by an ill informed voting public, influenced by their respective characteristics of social dominance, and politicians burdened with political ideology with less morals than financial obligation to support their self-interested well being. In order for any effort toward social control to be successful it must set parameters for levels of law enforcement performance based on degrees of requirement measuring degrees of safety, for the entire population above preferences of social grouping.

Society places law enforcement in an untenable position of addressing human behavior with strict rules of application. We might find ourselves variously at a point on a line which at one end throws human beings at great personal risk to themselves against irresponsible or contradictory human behavior, or at the other end restricting personal freedoms completely to assure security for all. Does the latter bring Orwellian utopia to mind? But, should law enforcers be so expendable as to follow demands of law and not supportive to community values they share a part of by virtue of their employment of choice?

"The Prince" in contemporary politics

Machiavelli provides an explanation for elite government power taking action to assure its high social dominance positions of responsibility. But while the sixteenth century Italian political philosopher claimed that leaders should not overlook the need to serve principles of justice for the citizens, he does provide a long-standing belief that those in charge should take all necessary steps to remain in power. Occasionally, it is necessary for those in power to break the law in order to protect and to promote "order," at least for an existing social dominance.

Is it difficult to accept the principle that, as former President Richard Nixon claimed, "when the president does it, it is not illegal."[117] This quotation appears to say, in the words of those in power, that what is called law is

---

[117] Interview with British journalist David Frost, found at, https://www.inquirer.com/philly/blogs/attytood/When-the-president-does-it-that-means-it-is-not-illegal.html

a flexible system of rules subject to interpretation by those who apply them, at least for the president. Although this contradicts words in the U.S. Constitution that only the Judicial Branch has such power, the Chief Executive may apply circumstantial meaning in applying principles of law, as meant to effect order. This suggests that political dominance in a society he/she is a member of defines the purpose of law and order. Meaning of law becomes fluid in addressing issues of conflict between different socially defining elements. But when administered by those in power, it gives an upper hand to the wealthy and members of majority groups who set the parameters for determining law and order.

A simple truth

One cannot contest the need for social order, at least from the perspective of the stronger element of social dominance. As a result, definition of what constitutes order is in question. If order follows laws of nature, society will perpetually be at odds with the controlling authority, no matter what social grouping exists. What seems missing in this consideration is circumstance. When the Supreme Court includes circumstance in its explanation of meaning it is accused of activism, making law from the bench. What value then remains for the conservative segments of society entrenched in strict definitions of acceptable social behavior? At what level of discourse in the Public Sphere can common values be determined such that social order could result as influence on political rules of law?

Dialogue 20. Democracy functioning in a representative state

Is there anyone in the United States who would not claim the government to be democratic? Or that he or she lives in a democracy? Or, that they wouldn't want other than a democracy?

A quick dictionary search presents democracy in modern usage as a system of government in which the citizens exercise power directly or indirectly through elect representatives from among themselves to form a governing body. Even in referring to democracy as was practiced in Classical Greece one finds it in reference to political representatives in government chosen by citizens (male and free), even if strictly through representatives.

Elements of democracy

According to political scientist Larry Diamond,118 democracy consists of four key elements: (1) A political system for choosing and replacing the government through free and fair elections; (2) Active participation of the people, as citizens, in politics and civic life; (3) Protection of human rights of all citizens, and (4) Rule of law, in which the laws and procedures apply equally to all citizens.

Consider the Preamble of the Constitution in which the application of democracy is framed for the United States. "We the people, in Order to form a more perfect Union, establish Justice, insure domestic Tranquility, provide

---

[118] Diamond, Larry J., In Search for Democracy, Routledge, 2016.

for the common defense (sic), promote the general Welfare, and secure the Blessings of Liberty to ourselves and our Posterity…"

Representatives to the House of Representatives, "…shall be composed of Members chosen every second Year by the People of the several States, and the Electors in each State shall have the Qualifications requisite for Electors of the most numerous Branch of the State Legislature." For this definition, one can accept that electors are active voters themselves, as there are no others representing directly the voters.

Representatives to the Senate, "… shall be composed of two Senators from each State, chosen by the Legislature thereof, for six Years; and each Senator shall have one Vote." We set aside the effects of the Seventeenth Amendment that gave citizens of each state the power to elect senators directly.

For election of the President, "Each State shall appoint, in such Manner as the Legislature thereof may direct, a Number of Electors, equal to the whole Number of Senators and Representatives to which the State may be entitled in the Congress . . .". It can be noted that the Twelfth Amendment restricted the Electoral College to vote for President and Vice President together, rather than splitting votes between candidates from different political parties. The Seventeenth Amendment also established the popular election of United States Senators directly by the people, as mentioned above.119

The Electoral College is pivotal in electing the President, as its original purpose was to create a buffer between voting power of the general population and voting power of States in the selection of an Executive leader. As is present in contemporary popular discourse, how then is the original con-

---

[119] Found at, https://constitutioncenter.org/interactive-constitution/amendment/amendment-xvii

struct for electing the President by Electoral College voting supportive of democracy favoring solely the choice of the people?

As claimed by those who support "original meaning" for the Constitution against claims of those with a contemporary interpretation of "living document" from the same intent, we have a disconnect. More specifically, we find in contemporary discussions the notion that the Electoral College might no longer have relevance for an election system for a democracy, apparently assuming that the democracy should directly reflect the voice of the people, with respect to selecting government leaders.

The same discussion was held as the Constitution was originally drafted. The dispute was between Federalists such as Alexander Hamilton and anti-Federalists such as Thomas Jefferson. The salient issue for the Federalists was that the electors would be able to ensure that only a qualified person becomes President. They believed that with the Electoral College no one would be able to manipulate the citizenry, a check on an electorate who might otherwise be duped. Hamilton and others did not trust the population to make the right choice, as was discussed in Federalist Paper #68.

Jefferson and his contemporaries supported the idea that leadership should be determined by the voice of the people, an idea emphasized by President Andrew Jackson some forty years later. How this voice should be weighed differs between the two individuals. Two conflicts appear. One addresses the different perspectives of the Framers; the other addresses different evolving perspectives of everyone since the Constitution was drafted until the present. The critical question remains: How should the President be elected to demonstrate a democracy responsive to both individuals and to the separate States?

A solution for electing the president

Following the concept of democracy outlined above, we can agree that the voice of the people should be heard in the election of a President. In supporting Jefferson's position aligned with State's rights and following original constitutional intent, elections by the citizens (directly or supported by voting electors) determine who represents them in government - hence the House of Representatives. Since the United States was formed as a union of States, each State should have a voice in determining the nature of a democratic government, consistent with limitations imposed by the U.S. Constitution.

States should determine their own members of the Senate. We can agree with this. However, to provide the citizens a direct voice in determining who would be Senators for their respective States and then have these respective States for these Senators vote directly for the President would duplicate the power of citizens who consequently would over-emphasize their choices against those of the State government where they live. We should note the result from the Seventeenth Amendment that changed the locus of power in electing the President. It moved from power shared between direct State voices (respective State officials) and individual citizen voting (House of Representatives) to only citizen voting power. States lost their respective individual voices in favoring citizen voting in determining how representation should occur under the Constitution.

Significantly, the purpose for the Electoral College was in compromising power between States power and citizens - as well as balancing disproportionate influence between large and small states. But that did not end attacks against the Electoral College, as some states decided to align their Electoral votes with results of the popular vote of the nation rather than with the results of state-wide voting. Effectively, this became an end-run around the Electoral College.

Some state legislatures passed laws agreeing to award their electoral votes to the candidate who wins the national popular vote. In doing so, there would be no practical value for the existence of the Electoral College, but effectively (even officially) abolishing the effect of the College only kicks in when enough states sign on to add up to 270 electoral votes. At the time of this writing, the ten states in such unofficial compact include: Hawaii, Illinois, Maryland, Massachusetts, New Jersey, Washington, Vermont, California, Rhode Island and New York.

Under the Compact Clause of the Constitution, "no state shall, without the consent of Congress enter into any agreement or compact with another state, or with a foreign power." According to Amy Sherman of Politifact, Florida, "courts have ruled that if federal supremacy is threatened, congressional consent is required for a compact to be valid."120 Nevertheless, with these states granting electoral votes to winners of the nation-wide presidential election, representative republic has a different meaning today than it did in 1787, and thus so does democracy.

Why not return to original intent, since that is where democracy was defined constitutionally. Individual citizens vote for their local representative in government (House of Representatives)? States, by whatever means thought appropriate to them, determine their representatives in government (Senate). A compromise between the two electoral bodies determines the Executive leader (President). Here are some benefits.

---

[120] This directive, known as the Compacts Clause, is found in Article I, Section 10, Clause 3 of the Constitution.

The government remains a democracy, because individual citizens determine directly or indirectly who serves as President. (Keep purpose of republic in mind.)

• Both State and citizen rights are served in keeping with the compromise reached between Federalists and anti-Federalists in drafting the Constitution.

• Conflict between popular vote and Electoral vote, such as occurred in 1828, 2000 and in 2016, would not be repeated because national voting for President would be represented state-wide rather than nation-wide.

• The effect of political parties would be reduced to influencing state-wide voting.

• National rhetoric would be limited with considerable reduction in demands for only wealthy candidates to compete.

• The voice of an influential media would be reduced in value, as its focus would be state-wide rather than nation-wide.

• Citizens would be disavowed of the belief that their power alone represents democracy in a republic.

• Candidates for presidency could come from any of multiple political ideologies appropriate to State interest rather than supporting a popularity contest.

• The President would be limited to address nation-wide and international issues rather than domestic ones more relevant to States.

To make it work, repealing parts of the Seventeenth Amendment would be necessary to restore States rights in the Constitutional Republic framed originally for the country. State electors might defer to how citizens in their respective states actually voted for a president in the national election, but only Electoral votes representing political views of the respective States (and not the nation as a whole) would count, contrary to the current proposed policy behind the National Popular Vote Bill. Passing this Bill would guarantee the presidency to the candidate who receives the most popular votes in all 50 states and the District of Columbia, in spite of constitutional power granted to the States to determine their own respective processes for voting in national elections.

A simple truth

The Electoral College does not need to be repealed. The original intent of the Constitution remains valid. Instead, repeal or replace the Seventeenth Amendment and remove the influence of political parties at the state level to assure citizen interests are served, rather than those of ideological groups which have their own political interests to support.

Keeping in mind that States have primary rights in amending the Constitution, begin the discussion for amassing interest in retaining original principle behind the Electoral College at a Public Sphere level where citizen voice has its greatest influence rather than allowing political party influence to take hold. Remember, there were no political parties in existence when the Electoral College was created. From the Public Sphere to State ballot boxes and public forums with elected State officials in attendance would carry the message of citizens. The risk is allowing political parties a voice in the process, particularly because political parties reflect a national perspective and not one necessarily favorable to States which might have their own differing political perspective.

Dialogue 21. Technology for democracy

With the expansion of smart telephone use and virtually ubiquitous presence of the Internet, more than half the world has access to or is aware of government behavior and services. In a democracy access through the Internet can provide real opportunity for citizens to participate in determining governance which serves them. With arrangement of citizen and access technology, service providers (government functionaries and their external partners) as a third element in the democratic process can be expected to maintain the same pace as demand for both information and access increases.

With rapidly growing sophistication of communication technology and related access to available information on government performance, slower progress of government's use of technologies contributes to growing disappointment. Cost related to technology expansion introduces problems of inadequate funding, not to mention shortage of internal technology experts to contribute to developing improved access, performance, as well as assuring quality in the information required for more appropriate service.

Is technology enough?

Citizens expect democracy and its agents - political parties and special interest groups, to support their participation in government, and to gain the best value from government service. It appears from contemporary rhetoric that more dialog on what democracy is and how it works may be needed, anticipating better understanding than is commonly assumed related to applications of technology. (Providing access to government does not in itself improve performance of government.)

Many of today's technology conferences claim a focus on how technology can improve democracy - as if meaning of democracy in some way could be considered a constant, with commonly understood purpose and thus accepted, prima facie, by all. Indeed, improvements could occur as a result of technology, but not without understanding what democracy is, fundamentally. After all, who could disagree that the world generally could benefit from changes in favor of greater democracy brought about worldwide through technology that improves access?

While many public discussions, panel and otherwise, focus on improvements to democracy gained through innovation at the service level (networks and devices), few discussions, including those between and among government officials, characterize democracy other than from the perspective of improving citizen support as a result of technology.

Focus on technology's potential to support democracy more appropriately belongs at the electoral level and not at the technology supplier level. The electoral level influences government leadership and bureaucratic behavior, the primary elements of democracy.

A discussion of technology in support of democracy naturally addresses government resulting from its processes. Here we find a major source of confusion. Differentiation must be made between government as determined by a political process and governance as defined by what the political process of democracy provides. Supporting technologies serving the two are different. Perspectives exist that technologies that support functions of government (intra- and extra-agency) and those supporting the process of governance (how government serves the citizen) are different due to different levels of security required. Other perspectives claim that the same protection for security exist for both behaviors, but it is only different access that must be addressed.

The government environment

The level of citizen involvement in government processes determines the amount of attention devoted to the use of technology for government. Generally, the more active citizens are in government, the greater the interest in how technology is used to support their activities.

Democracy from a constitutional perspective addresses how government can be formed and what its interactive behavior should be. In proscribing democracy one focuses on how citizens vote to determine government leadership and then influence the determination of what government does once formed. Up until the present, citizens world-wide have demonstrated less influence in determining what democratic government does, leaving this to the legislative function resulting from elected leadership. After all, this is the intended value of a republic - taking the responsibility for government out of the hands of uninformed citizens and placing it in the hands of experts.

The politics behind democratic government should not be assumed as merely a process, viewed only in terms of results of its performance. Voting and all other citizen forms of participation follow ideological influence. Leadership results from expression of a majority ideology or coalition of multiple ideologies with common agreement for overlapping interests. What governance of such leadership creates in the name of citizen values reflects these same ideological influences.

A place for technology

While technology can support the determination of leadership such that equal access to voting is accommodated, it must be just as neutral in supporting access to programs resulting from the legislative process. But, democracy results only if citizen participation is successful. As a result of openness of access, a majority political ideology of voters finds its way into governance. Under democracy, once government is determined, influential citizen participation in how democracy is rolled out appears limited to the supporting political ideologies of elected leaders, or indeed removing these political leaders.

Discussing how technology can support democracy at the governance level occurs whether or not the government is democratic. After all, government could follow a different model, such as autocratic or totalitarian. Here access technology would be less supported than technologies supporting intra-agency communication and information processing.

As education is claimed important in understanding democracy and how technology could be applied to improve governance developed under a framework of democracy, one might consider how those who claim to serve the interests of democracy specific to technological advancement might gain better value through "tightening up" their concepts, through both development and presentation.

If technology is promoted for its own sake, all well and good. Better that it not attempt to ride the coat tails of a commercial concept not well aligned with democratic values, or values held by government functionaries. Government, and specifically democracy, might be better served if it were the focus for developing technology as a supportive element. Consideration for what is uniquely government and under what code of ethics democracy is to be formed would not have to anticipate problems related to efficiency and effectiveness of products competing in the public domain. Both perspectives are critical to technology developers, but cost structures for different development methods should be accommodated.

Technology as a liability

As with many elements of government, a high degree of trust is needed to both assure access and quality of service received. What is thought to be true must be shown to be true, in some understandable way. Additionally, protection of personal data embedded in government services should not be cause for concern of risk from compromise or misuse. Things such as personal identities should be as they are reported to be. How they are used is a different issue.

Democratic government must keep pace with its regulated community. Technological advances in healthcare, transportation, safety and other industries provide improved service to citizens. As regulated entities these same industries require government understanding of capabilities and liabilities in order to regulate good practice for the good of society. This is evidence-based theory.

Political ideological differences existing naturally in any society are fed by citizen proponents more interested in supporting their own personal beliefs and demands than considering value for the community at large. When information is communicated with the purpose of undermining others as a primary objective rather than in supporting common human goals, distortions and disinformation corrupt value in communication serving only its own purpose.

As increasing success is gained through technological expansion, economies of scale are pursued. What was once considered as an extreme element of science fiction, Isaac Asimov's fictional "Multivac" could arrive, as it seems already to exist in the application of cloud computing.121

Whether of not management and control of virtually all information used to support human behavior is appropriate, accountability seems to be in short supply. For example, Google's ability to store any and all information has led to uncertainty of quality for the information retrieved from storage, a similar claim by the academic community against use of Wikipedia.

In short, it is not the anticipated value in accessing information that should be of interest, it is assurance of quality in both the technology infrastructure for accessing and storing information, as well as the use of information itself, that warrant deliberate attention.

A simple truth

Information should be neutral; that is, it exists as a free element identifying and explaining life and living. How it is used gives it operational value, distorted to reflect the interests of both the developer and the user. With growing use of and dependence on social networks for information, risk of distortion of intended purpose easily occurs. When information is used to limit or denigrate common moral beliefs, the technology can be questioned by a protective government. The moral principles can remain in the Public Sphere where they are inspected and evaluated through debate for effectiveness of the human condition.

---

[121] Multivac was the name of a fictional supercomputer appearing in several science fiction novels by Isaac Asimov. Its concept was also presented as Hal-9000 in Arthur Clarke's Space Odyssey series.

Dialogue 22. Transitioning sovereignty

In thinking of sovereignty we imagine the specter of an element seemingly with spiritual power that both guides and controls us. A government claims sovereignty, and within the government a single executive leader often claims sovereignty by appearing to control the process of governing.

Is a spiritual element necessarily sovereign in guiding the government leader? In a democratic government, in which citizens are claimed to have primary power, what role does or should spirituality play in influencing government leaders? Is spirituality the source of real sovereignty since it can occur either through controlling behavior of citizens or effecting influence on the leader?

Which recipient of influence from spirituality embodies sovereignty? Machiavelli (1469-1527) claimed the latter. What should it be? How can we know the real source of sovereignty such that a majority could support its validity?

For too long a time democracy has suffered through contradictory notions about what its proper role is, how it is supposed to perform that role, and to what extent it should demonstrate its constitutional sovereignty outwardly. Does government control the people only through inherent sovereignty, or are the people who follow a spiritual sovereignty in charge of controlling government?

Part of the difficulty in the United States from such pairing of ambiguities is the language provided in the U.S. Constitution.122 Does the Constitution rule out influence from a sovereignty through different spiritual beliefs of citizens? Or does the Constitution allow that spirituality could arrive through citizen beliefs and thus occupy an indirect role of sovereignty?

From the weight of the Bill of Rights, the first ten constitutional amendments added in 1791, the focus for democracy appeared to rest on rights for and in support of citizens. Less attention for the Bill of Rights, although tacitly assumed by the Framers in the Tenth Amendment, was the stability of government, moving as it did from supporting power of the individual states as under the Articles of Confederation to supremacy of central power.

Focus of government action during this period lay clearly on the side of preserving central power. Why not, claim supporters? After all, as noted much earlier by Machiavelli, later by Thomas Hobbes, and more recently by Giorgio Agamben,123 government must survive in order to support citizens. The issue of sovereignty seemed not in question for these individuals. It wasn't until Andrew Jackson (U.S. President from 1829-1837) that the earlier focus on centralizing power shifted to acknowledging power of citizens, however sovereignty resulted with this new focus. Not much has changed since then.

For the United States, the first major challenge to sovereignty in democracy existed between power of the central government as witnessed in the Constitutional Convention during 1788 and power inherent with the people at the State level. More recently, change in the preponderance of action re-

---

122 Enterprise Clause in the First Amendment

123 See Agamben, Giorgio, Homo Sacer: Sovereign Power and Bare Life, Standford Univ. Press, 1998.

garding location of power took place with the Civil War in an effort to strengthen central government against sovereign power of state level governments. Rights of the citizens was relegated circumstantially to play only tacitly as source of sovereign power.

A significant refocusing of sovereignty in government was influenced in 1962 when Rachel Carson produced "Silent Spring," based on scientific work performed during the 1950's.124 Considering the scope of concern for affects on the environment from government, industry and even individuals, supremacy over either government or citizen action in a democracy was challenged by the dominant role credited to the environment.

To what extent the impact of environmental concern occurred was heightened in 2006 by "An Inconvenient Truth" credited to Al Gore.125 Largely from this work a major claim for supremacy for the environment began. It considered health of the entire planet as a single focus for source of sovereignty. The environment is influenced by actions of both government with its supported industries, and from individual behaviors of citizens. (Lesser influence is cited from nature, and from animal forms living in nature.)

With attention on the environment, government attention takes on a new focus, a third element in the power base for determining how democracy is to be justified and supported. Against dispute between state power and citizen power in determining the supremacy of democracy, the fictional three-

---

[124] Carson, Rachel, Silent Spring, Houghton Mifflin, Boston, 2003.

[125] "An Inconvenient Truth" is a documentary film developed by the former Vice President.

headed Ghidorah126 took form as an extraterrestrial imperative, and with it a different perspective.

The application of conflict

Nowhere is the three-way demand for supremacy in democracy more pronounced than in current political activities in France. What began as a public concern for government taxation of citizens in the form of higher prices on automobile fuel was revealed to show government action to support environmental concern for air pollution. The claimed political justification to reduce exhaust contaminants masked intent for limiting use of automobiles.

The French government found itself in an indefensible position. In claiming to practice democracy the government presents itself with a heavy bias toward citizen service, essentially framing politics along socialistic lines. At the present time, France was taking steps to adjust its socialist focus to become an international player by strengthening its support for environmental stability. So long as the government can find a fiscal means to support its espoused emphasis on environmental concerns, citizens have accepted higher tax rates (roughly 55.7 percent tax contribution consisting of value-added tax and tax on income in 2016).

In order to support such a large federal system for social benefits (approximately 30 percent of GDP compared with 16 percent of GDP in the United States), France depends on contributions from taxed business growth in the private sector, and programmatically supports it. As in the United

---

126 The three-headed King Ghidorah shows up in Japanese culture to defeat the combined forces of Godzilla, Rodan, and Mothra.

States, industry contributors to environmental degradation are taxed at higher rates than individual consumers.

Up to the present time in France, a reasonable balance occurs between government support for social service in acceptance of sovereign responsibility with citizens and support for environment stewardship in supporting the State as an international player. The current French President, Emmanuel Macron, exercises a leadership role in supporting programs dealing with environmental stewardship. Thus, support for environment, and for self-promotion as a world leader, moves beyond government's traditional sovereign domain.

But the present time also presents effects of an intruding concern for economic matters. By increasing taxing support to government, allowances for private sector investment have taken priority over concerns for citizen support. The reaction by citizen sectors was demonstration against State claims to support environmental stewardship with tax dollars. What originated as claims against unjustified automobile fuel tax increase born by citizens morphed into a more general concern for economic imbalance between citizens and the government policy toward environmental protection. In this way, the sovereign role for the environment was challenged by citizen resistance to taxation by the State.

The violent citizen reaction known as gilet jaune[127] in France began in December 2018 when a large number of French citizens influenced government leaders to reconsider the path it was taking to address this third source of sovereign influence. As a reasonable proposal at the time, rescinding fuel tax increases in favor of higher wealth tax, including for property owners, would stave off concerns against environmental support. Alas, attack on

---

[127] yellow vest

economic stability for citizens redistributes attention from the lower income brackets to the higher income brackets.

What seems clear is that economic concerns in a democratic government would not change. The State must be fully funded. The environment's potential for imposing its sovereignty over government would be unchallenged as long as the defining issue of sovereignty itself is balanced between the State and its citizens, depending on who is required to underwrite larger costs for environmental stewardship and tax bills.

Effects of a third sovereignty

Effectively, manipulation of citizen taxation as example of how the State retains sovereignty against imposed environmental concerns would not change the emphasis on democracy other than on how wealth is to be redistributed. This element of Social Contract is thus preserved. Sovereignty in support of democracy remains consistent with the stability of government, and that requires satisfying claims of citizens for better and fair service. Economic balance toward environmental stewardship rather than serving citizens changes focus for sovereignty. Are citizens in positions of sovereign power to claim for clean air and pure water? Is the government sovereign in the steps it takes to assure environmental stability? Or, are both under the implicit influence of the environment in the way it "demands" support from government, from industry that supports government and citizens, or from citizens?

Concern for environmental stewardship could affect all three elements of sovereignty, but extent is undetermined. They are not likely to change the current balance between government control and citizen support unless State relinquishes its obligation to support a healthy, uncontaminated environment. A greater oversight role could provide environment stewardship through a central international government focused specifically and fully on the environment, very unlikely in contemporary norms of democracy.

A simple truth

The issue of sovereignty may be a false issue. What appears to be of greater concern for citizens is their well being. For the State it is supremacy to make and enforce law. When both citizen and State concerns are satisfied, attention is turned to the environment, or to an undefined spiritual influence expanding the notion of environment. Claiming sovereignty for the latter indicates either or both former sovereign roles are under-supported. Level of concern for the environment seems highly correlated with agreement between citizens and the State over the role of government in caring for the environment. Social stability exists when citizens are satisfied by government support to the environment, and thus, government retains its self-sustaining sovereign power.

Dialogue 23. Lacking as ideal, democracy does exist

The world has many examples of claimed democracy in practice. From the Russian Federation to the United States case studies demonstrate how democracy functions: well, not so well, and poorly in some applications. We might take encouragement for the future of democracy were it not the case that current applications of democracy do not offer a standard for comparing all of democracy, nor all democracies. Without a standard there is no effective comparison to determine improvement toward an ideal.

No version of claimed democracy represents through its practices to be based on classical liberal political philosophy. Not only has influence from the likes of Locke and Rousseau been misleading for contemporary democratic principles, but those of democracy's founders, considering Jefferson and Madison, are set aside in favor of principles more closely aligned with direct democracy than representative democracy. We can turn to an even earlier political thinker, Thomas Hobbes, who considered the role and dangers of democratic thought as influenced by voters to be anathema to classical liberal thinking during that period.

The single most influential element contradictory to the liberal foundation of democracy is, ironically, the very element of its focus. Democracy is a form of government intended to support the people. From the people, increasingly, selection of representative leadership has slipped into populism. While populism in itself cannot be blamed for any problem with democracy, the fact that choice of leadership has been corrupted by a sense that people are capable of determining leadership based on no more than public awareness and popular acceptance of the candidate who happens to promise what captures the interests of citizens.

The issue of direct popular determination for leadership today arguably began in the United States with the election of John F. Kennedy as a popular favorite for president over the more stable claims of institutional stability under Richard M. Nixon. More than any political qualification Kennedy brought with him into office, he was popular based on many elements not related to presidency, such as elite family structure and fresh ideas as supporting "a time of greatness."

The press can be blamed only partially, as its support to Richard Nixon, the Republican challenger and heir apparent to the Dwight Eisenhower presidency, seemed to run against public sentiment. More populist support was emphasized for growing personal power in the White House than feeding a democracy built of leaders who promoted political ideals. Here, we can see the main difference between politically qualified Nixon and then President Dwight Eisenhower who gained popular support as a result of a successful military campaign to end World War II.

The maturation of populism grew rapidly from the Eisenhower presidency, stemming from the campaign slogan, "I Like Ike." Eisenhower's appeal was based on building stability against fears from ideological difference advanced by the Soviet Union. Appreciation for his charisma and personality resulted from a popular Administration that attempted to bring different cultures together under one nation. People were soon to begin understanding that the political process for electing representative officials had followed an outdated sense of how democracy could support political ideology. Voting for a single executive could be oriented more to popular national stability than in deference to a less interesting claim for democratic principles and political ideology difference.

Popularized elements of leadership personality soon after became the primary characteristic for what voters believed supportive of them, only vaguely echoing claims of democracy. Since the anchors of democracy lay deeply in the ideals of support to the people, a new interpretation of support to the people lay in how democracy supports voices for personal appeal. This evolutionary rethinking opened up media to the opportunity to build support (and readership) based more on personal appeal of candidates than on political qualifications for office.

That anyone should doubt the validity of this claim for populist support, consider the stream of presidents since Kennedy and his Vice President following him into office. Re-election bid loss from lack of personal appeal in claims for environmental stewardship of Jimmy Carter to the populist Ronald Reagan, whose appeal was based on popularity from successful careers in Hollywood and television, and a political license as governor resulting from California's populism. A virtually unknown governor from Arkansas, but soon to become popular nationally, gained support from voters in resistance to re-election of a candidate with strong anchors in the CIA (the contributing source for some claims of involvement in the assassination of President Kennedy) and an unfavorable position with voters due to his penchant for military expedition in Panama - Bush's later military success in Iraq notwithstanding. With the close of the Clinton period, and due to powerful political machinery at the time exposed by the demonized Electoral College, uncharismatic Al Gore was not successful in defeating G.W. Bush. Later popular support for Bush while in office was lessened by a popular war chant publicized by a populist-fed media machine. There can be no question that the next two presidential elections, Barack Obama and Donald Trump, were examples of populism in practice.

But the succession of popular individuals to the presidency is not the only element to consider in citing a transition to populist democracy. Demands for popular choice of voters offer further support for unraveling the Electoral College. The Seventeenth Amendment in 1913 that transferred determination of Senators from respective state legislatures to direct determination by voters was not enough. Increasingly, influence for government leadership positions through personal appeal rather than through political credentials seems more relevant to voters. Appeal for allowing indirect voting overseen by the State through the Electoral College is waning. State interests are overridden by citizen choice.

Democracy today in the United States

For those who continue to believe that the practice of democracy in the United States today is the same as the democracy implicit in the U.S. Constitution, consider how meaning for "government of the people, by the people" has changed in application since it appeared in Lincoln's Gettysburg Address during the American Civil War in 1863.

Is democracy a concept or an operation? Is today's practice of democracy really what was intended by the U.S. Constitution? It all depends on what role is intended for the people whose support is thought protected. Answers appear to favor influence from populism. If only voters' choices could be trusted to favor more than popular appeal.

Can it be that democracy is no more than government supporting citizen expectations of having all they need to survive and otherwise to be left alone? The little bit more than that begs a desire to grow and develop as part of an ideal. It is the space where the Public Sphere has great effects in improving democracy.

A simple truth

As for a vague and misleading issue of sovereignty, the notion of democracy suffers from lack of maturity for action from an ideal. Democracy might well exist in the world, for the United States and elsewhere, where practice is capable potentially of satisfying citizen concerns for satisfying life's basic requirements: adequate food, shelter, and safety. Being left alone from government imposition would also qualify as satisfying citizen concerns. A government "in the face" of citizens lacks public appeal. Democracy claimed by any candidate who campaigns to reduce pressure from government could qualify to populist citizens, even without the trapping of a Bill of Rights.

Being left alone provides citizens ample opportunity to solve their own life problem issues. It also provides the opportunity to share ideals without regulated control, when the press is free to carry messages. Through development of ideals in the Public Sphere, more effective discussions and debates could become manifest for defining effective government, rather than pandering to social networks supporting populist leaders. That could move democracy from ideal to practice.

Dialogue 24. Can media be trusted to be objective?

In referring to the media, we have in mind collectively the functions of journalism. The public could expect the media to present different types of information objectively, leaving it up to the readers or viewers to determine subjective value.

One of the first functions for media in the United States was to present the views of government leaders. George Washington and his colleagues were regular contributors to reported news, even as biased as it was to those who fed information directly to the press. Today, this partisan journalism is open to anyone interested in presenting a point of view. And, it is not limited to government leaders. Channels are open for individuals or groups to present positions in anticipation of or searching for support. As activities progress along the political spectrum media is expected to report it as signalers to the public of current events. An additional type of reporting occurs when the press investigates political issues to inform readers of problems and progress.

Read or view any item from popular media sources, such as The Washington Post, the New York Times, or CNN, and a video recording can present to the interested reader the essence of the story reported. The reader can avoid the video in favor of reading the details, and may find substantial information different from that presented in the video material. In a sense, what the text provides is a detailed view of material presented in the attention grabbing video, full descriptions to generate or to support pre-existing interest.

Media transforms content through personalization in an effort to attract readership already motivated to search for news, or who wants simply to be entertained. With each news item a miniature theatrical presentation built around events of interest can be experienced. This constitutes news and panders to the appeal of readers whose voting interest is based on how well the presentation of news can be entertaining or just gains attention. The process feeds the voyeuristic penchant of those whose attention otherwise might be devoted to watching television stars such as Oprah Winfield, sports celebrities such as LeBron James, or Hollywood attractions such as Robert DeNiro. Financially endowed commercial entities provide the professionalism building appeal for the viewer, such that less well developed and less attractive material lacks viewer interest and thus has less influence.

Compare the different levels of appeal from video presentations of video news and the straight text presentations of Foreign Policy or Truthout. Who bothers with the latter two, when the same topics can be presented in a frame of biasing entertainment. Viewers of popular commercial news outlets correlate with the voting public, at least as a populist majority.

Where we are today

It might be of interest to note the current multi-topic disputes between the President of the United States with the conservative news reporting sources, arguably a populist leaning grouping, and major liberal media sources. The topics of interest are in common, and wrapping of content is done in similar ways to gain respective support from the public, or to reinforce it. Their mutual success in this parade of contentious issues is based on the same social elements found only in attention seeking reporting. The irony is that they position themselves to be different by claiming each other to be sources of "fake news."

Issues found in headline seeking reporting typically represent biased personal opinion or are related to populist actions of elected leadership. The same issue might be reported by more objective sources, but these sources provide explanation and details for support, not of interest to headline followers. They might reflect legitimacy by claiming to be objective through contradiction to more overtly biased sources.

Expectations for objective journalism are minimal in the public perspective due to lack of interest in material contradictory to personal opinion, other than for socially marginalized intellectuals. That is, objective journalism lacks entertainment value.

Subscription expectations by serious, objective sources are often needed due to lack of corporate financial backing. Organizations such as Truthout and Web versions of Foreign Policy expect viewers to pay for access to their news services. Even the New York Times and The Washington Post expect financial support for web material to be subscriber supported. Populist media sources, such as Fox News, are funded by corporations which expect sales components of the media to result in financial gain, or that support for candidates is justified through favorable public opinion polls.

But whether sources are objective or not, the presentation of news reflects the reader's orientation to being entertained, emotionally or intellectually. Hence, financial support is sought by advertisers who gain from access to reader interests. The majority of demand for news arrives from populist views of readers. It all but prevents the existence of objectivity in commercial media. Since the early days of journalism has this ever been different?

A simple truth

One might conveniently differentiate between types of journalism and regard purpose for journalism as significant to value of material, but to the extent any objectivity could result from consuming news depends on the reader. Does the reader expect the source to provide objectivity such that truth could be revealed directly by the material exposed? Isn't this the responsibility of the reader and not the source? Are issues subject to debate, or are they merely wrapped in biased attempts to gain acceptance and support without need to research presented material. Has the purpose in seeking truth stated by Socrates been lost in the rush for subjective value emphasized in populism rather than objectivity?

Part III: Humanity - The nature of human existence seems to sit between two concepts: who we are and what we do.

There exists an idea that with technology taking over the functions of the human more advanced living would result. That leaves us with two questions. Are humans held back from their potential in life for lack of technology? And, if all we do can be accomplished by some form of digital automation, does that explain to us that we are what we do and not who we are?

Including technology and its impact in public discourse provides a dimension of pragmatism that advances the value of meaning for individual human behavior. Argumentative discourse following Habermas and Apel with its essential normative presuppositions is fundamental for justifying claims raised in debate.128

Some individuals are disposed to accept that the role of government is to provide for the citizen those elements not possessed in the normal course of living. That might suggest, at least for these individuals, basic elements of living are inadequate to serve the interests of humanity. There must be more. Pleonexia, Plato called it. We seek "more" through sharing thoughts and understandings in order to arrive at common meaning for humanity as a result of debate.

---

[128] See contrasting discussion in Gamwell, Franklin, Habermas and Apel on communicative ethics: Their difference and the difference it makes, Philosophy and Social Criticism, 1997.

Dialogue 25. A question of knowing

During our entire conscious existence we gain information about ourselves, about others, and about our environment. Is all we learn dependent on, or determined by, what we are taught? Taught by others? Taught by experience? Is the human a sponge, an existence of absorbent material that collects experiences of life as they are presented? Does the human enter life in the state of tabula rasa? John Locke claimed in his "Essay Concerning Human Understanding" that people enter life with a blank mind. That might be so, but is human understanding limited to functions of the mind?

Interdependence

Often in life we are exposed to the explanation that a progressive relationship beginning with signals and ending with wisdom explains the path for understanding things. This progression may be viewed differently than from a continuous linear time line of learning. Comprehension of new ideas and awareness of transformation toward future states of existence requires something catalytic, something external to the process of learning, even while facilitating it. The linear transformational relationship from signals to data to information to knowledge to wisdom seems to just happen serendipitously, as if understanding is inherent in awareness.

Two different elements appear to contribute to awareness of the transformation from signal to wisdom. One is the existence of observable things, the substance of knowledge. The second element is the energy that facilitates awareness, the causation for each iterative transition. Would it be possible otherwise that any stage becomes the next through serendipity or spontaneity, requiring no conscious or extra-conscious enablement? Paradoxically, could it be that new energy is created from each transformation, leading to the causation for each new stage, following a Casimir–Polder relationship for moving atoms?129 What might be the energy source that initiates the first movement in thought, or even subsequently during life?

Is all that we know defined by what we are taught, what we learn from experience and from observing others? What do we know that is not so acquired? If all we know, or can know, is taught to us, does nothing exist which is not already known, forming the only shape for what is to be taught? Is there nothing new? Is there not something external to our thinking that stimulates new thought?

Have we as a species not advanced in knowledge beyond Socrates, diverging along the movement from the single immutable force of Aristotle to gain maturity in authority through understanding? Does Plato's Scala Natura, further developed by Aristotle include more than authority the human species gains through understanding in a Great Chain of Being above other animals?130 Is instinct not the energy that separates humans from animals in permitting creation of new thought, something lacked by predecessors for what we know?

If we can know what is, what exists, through education and experience couldn't we also through another source for knowing understand what is not, what does not already exist? Is the level of knowledge we possess in-

---

129 The relationship demonstrates that the vacuum found between two elements of quantum field theory contain the energy for transforming one state to the other.

130 The Great Chain of Being, or *scala naturæ,* is a classical conception of the sequencing of maturity in the universe. Transition for all beings moves from the most basic to the most sophisticated or "perfect" hierarchically linked to form one interconnected whole.

creasing such that we are reducing the amount of knowledge we don't yet possess? Is there an asymptotic endpoint?

Assuming knowledge does not exist in the new-born, is attaining knowledge spontaneous with experience, or is there a stimulus from an energy outside knowledge that causes it to exist? Does the maturity of humanity depend on more than education through what Arthur Lovejoy described as the Great Chain of Being?131 What is the starting point for knowledge? What is the first signal in the linear chain leading to wisdom? Finally, on the other end of the spectrum does something beyond wisdom exist?

Perhaps it is just as reasonable to believe that the newborn carries energy from before birth that causes transformation of signals to knowledge. It could be this energy that possesses the element necessary for maturation, for attaining an advanced position not just above animals but above other humans on the way to "perfection." Plotinus in his Six Enneads132 referred to a superabundance of other ways to arrive at perfection resulting from attaining a stage of needing nothing further.

A simple truth

Claiming to know anything depends on understanding observable elements. Knowing the essence of something observable requires linear connection with things already verified and thus known, from theory that frames anticipation of testable knowledge and an energy less understood that supports growth in understanding. Can it be disputed that such energy follows

---

131 Lovejoy, Arthur, The Great Chain of Being: A Study of the History of an Idea, Harvard Univ. Press, 1936.

132 Discussed at http://classics.mit.edu/Plotinus/enneads.html

the vacuum relationship for pushing atoms in space, or from a mysterious force growing from Plotinus's sequence of gaining understanding?

We don't expect to know or to understand such things. We can however discuss them, and thus gain some collectivity of what is known. How else could we agree on any form of knowledge? We don't see nor understand everything surrounding knowledge. Neither do other individuals. Together, however, the total of all awareness through discussion could present a reality not otherwise knowable. That's a function of the Public Sphere.

Dialogue 26. Renewal of Respect for life

Respect for life is so general a topic for debate that it could take all means available to reflect centrality of one's own existence to determine relevance at the expense of considering centrality of another person who might pose a challenge from a different centrality that person might claim. Of course, life is not unique to the human, nor even unique in considering other forms than animals. Very simply, life is something that exists, and we, along with other forms, are representations of it. Lack of respect for the living element in any form of life is to disrespect life, itself.

The perspective of democracy

Poised at the beginning of each new year, one might expect commencement of better times. In spite of hope assigned in previous beginnings dissipating into empty annual dust, one dares to hope for renewed respect for human life, following events such as during September 11, 2001 at home and abroad. May citizen behavior against others produce better results than have occurred since then.

One issue of perennial concern is the uncontrolled behavior of individuals intent on using firearms against others for unexplainable, mostly irrational, purposes. At the beginning of 2012, then U.S. President Barack Obama vowed that a new task force overseen by Vice President Joe Biden would provide 'concrete proposals' by the end of January to reduce gun violence, a worthy effort for the sake of protecting lives. The motivation toward regulations on gun use resulted in part from an elementary school shooting in Newtown, Connecticut.133 It was not the first nor last gun related violence for the country, suggesting that a democracy representing value for citizens was not being realized as originally envisioned.

In addition to considering new laws to control gun acquisition and use, the Biden task force was expected to look at mental health care and what the President described as a culture that "glorifies guns and violence."134 Guns have an inextricable connection with death - the only absolute solution for fear, either for the individual or for the whole of society. A provoking shroud is cast by the Second Amendment of the U.S. Constitution that protects the right of all American citizens to keep and bear arms. The odds are thus unfavorable for effective gun control.

As most thinking going into the drafting of the Constitution evolved from social policies originating in Great Britain, language reflected cultural and social traditions thus inherited when the states together won their independence as a nation in 1776. Rationale of the subsequent Bill of Rights element was to restore "ancient rights" trampled upon by James II when Protestants threatened a Catholic oligarchy.135

At the root of concern for individual rights was fear of tyranny, fear that any ruling body could suppress any expression of discontent with the status quo. Justification found a new interpretation for constitutional rights in es-

---

133 Sandy Hook school shooting discussed at, https://www.history.com/this-day-in-history/gunman-kills-students-and-adults-at-newtown-connecticut-elementary-school.

134 CBS Video: "The stories we tell matter," Obama says a year after Sandy Hook shootings, Nov 26, 2013, found at, https://www.cbsnews.com/video/obama-tells-hollywood-not-to-glorify-gun-violence/

135 At issue at the time (1662) was resistance to repression of citizen groups by hierarchies of church leaders, Catholic and Protestant.

tablishment of a militia, inasmuch as there was no federal authority, nor even means, to build a national military.

The meaning of what supported this constitutional right in post-colonial times seems to have been lost across a few centuries during which the fear of despotic government (Church or State) was replaced by a contemporary perspective enabled by the Supreme Court decision in District of Columbia v. Heller136 that although the original justification for right to bear arms was no longer relevant, the provision for implied self protection remained. No such distinction for ownership as appeared in District of Columbia v. Heller appears in the constitutional amendment.

The irony is that a right to protect lives (against the malevolent hands of tyrannical government) became a circumstantial implement to take lives when other than government posed a threat against perceived personal liberty.

Citizen ownership of guns is not an easy issue to address when the question of protection of life is considered, never mind the quick responses many have to the question. Can taking any life be justified if saving another life is assured?

Nevertheless, we shouldn't pass over the inherent danger of firearms, of any kind. For this reason, we talk of imposing some level of gun control, both on ownership and on use. And, at the same time, we try to be supportive of the ideals inherent in the Constitution, for the sake of what we claim is protecting practice of citizen rights under democracy.

Here is where it gets difficult for many. Who should have such control? Who can be trusted with it other than government? Yet, it was untrustworthy

---

[136] District of Columbia v. Heller, 554 U.S. 570 (2008).

government that caused the need for citizen ownership of firearms in the first place. Does the individual really want government to know what firearms are owned, either to share such knowledge or to use it to deprive the individual of the right oof possession?

But, there is more to the issue. Owning a firearm can be considered a hobby, of sorts. In one way it is like collecting antique furniture, or repairing old automobiles. In a contradictory way, unlike owning furniture or automobiles, it poses a threat to life, when used in other than a manner of collection.

We also include the role firearms use plays in hunting, another aspect of freedom resulting from a time when survival depended on success in the wilderness, or fishing, or farming. Taken all together, we see in several ways how preserving an earlier right transitioned to supporting a different rationalization for use under that right. This transition is not unconstitutional. What gets messy is when a constitutional right of possession collides with another constitutional obligation to preserve life.

The ongoing issue before both the White House and the Congress continues to be in how to defend one constitutional right which threatens another right. Both sides in this debate generate tomes of argument with specious support to solidify a personal position resulting more from socialization than from an issue fundamental to human rights. Additionally, one finds intruding influence from an industry group claiming to defend any imaginable element of gun ownership while enhancing economic growth as further justification for the evolved interpretation of the Second Amendment right.

Where does protection for the right to bear arms overturn protection of the right to life, for the individual as well as for all others? Right to life is fundamental to all constitutional protections, and it is supported by what is believed a natural right of all people imbedded in the liberalism anchoring the U.S. Constitution.

And abroad, is the challenge to right of life for citizens of one nation, or even the nation itself, with regard to possession of life-ending technology, challenged just because its use is feared while at the same time touting its value in defending against aggressive acts of foreign governments? Such cold war mentality has prevailed since technology of total annihilation was applied against the Japanese in 1945. The mentality continues today through threats from use of such technology, as well as through developing such technology, dominating policy for international relations.

A basis for challenging rights to life

What reasonable approach exists for resolving conflict between protecting life and taking it? Is protecting life really preeminent to all other things. Life is really the only thing humans can call their own as a species, both as stewards to protect it and beneficiaries of it. Yet, protecting life seems synonymous with taking it under conditions of defense.

Hindu teaching provides one resolution through belief that life continues after death. The value of life to others is determined by how life is performed while it is experienced, with purpose as a justification for existence. This elevates the value of human life above that of other animals as well as above other life forms. The Catholic tradition characterizes meaning of life in terms of judgment following death. Each proposes that taking any life destroys the ability of the individual to accomplish value during existence. Both perspectives argue against taking another life as it prevents development or application of value for others.

A modest hope for any New Year resolution could suggest that respecting life would apply to the individual as well as to neighbors, here and abroad. If legislation is required to support such hope, how it is administered would suggest how much respect for life is to be found at the base of democracy. One might also accept that reducing fear could reduce anticipated need for protection. Part of reducing fear is ending the creation of it.

A simple truth

Claiming to respect life carries a huge burden for many in a democracy. Fear of death or bodily harm suggests a need to protect life. It demands justification for ownership of the means to terminate life. Equally, one might claim falsely generating fear, or generating false fear, to be anathema to democratic values. As an alternative to protecting against fear, perhaps a more reasonable approach is to learn how to live with fear.

Who discusses fear, these days? When do gun ownership supporters engage in discussion with those opposed to gun ownership? Indeed, when does debate center on the existence or value of life, now or beyond? Does value of life reach the same moral level as the Second Amendment right? Shouldn't it?

Dialogue 27. Women's rights

Throughout much of the nineteenth and twentieth centuries in the United States women such as Abigail Adams, the Grimké sisters, Elizabeth Cady Stanton, and the late Betty Friedan contributed to a movement to enhance respect for the female gender, if not respect for its position in society. In some cases they were aided by sympathetic males, but such support must be regarded as marginal because the issue of repression continued. While political influence created the most stir in public discourse, no doubt the issue of discrimination lay as well in other dealings in which the genders found themselves in stratified roles, with women subordinate to men.

In support of debate

At some point in the history of civilization, difference between male and female gender was acknowledged outside the sexual role of each, and from the subsequent complementary roles of mother and father. Inasmuch as nothing in our intellectual processes can alter this accounting we are obligated to search a different makeup to determine why gender role dispute exists. But certainly there should be no discounting of difference in considering how societal roles, beyond the family, might better suit political purposes in a democracy.

Much of the debate these days is on lack of compatibility between levels of compensation for what appears to have a basis in same pay for same performance. But the framework for such debate is based on the results of sociological development over centuries of behavior. Little argument can result by considering a different starting point. Yet, beginning from where society finds itself may be the problem for any debate. And, society finds itself a result of how the two genders and their respective roles vis-a-vis the family have transformed them.

Gender role debate might follow one of two paths. Either society should provide a means for the two different genders to behave similarly and to receive fair compensation proportional to effort, or society could be transformed to parallel the roles taken within the family. The latter debate might be more rational, but it doesn't seem the direction of contemporary claims by the female for equal treatment. What are found in various forms of social and literary media are claims that women deserve equal rights to positions of influence in society, that the two genders are equal in all respects and qualify for duty and equal compensation for equal performance.

Not much rhetoric addresses the nature of societal positions that result in some form of compensation. Specifically these roles were created from the thinking of men ages ago and how men saw order in society, with an emphasis on control. As has been reported often in literature, society is analogous to the family unit, with the advisory that structure in the family could work well in the larger societal unit. So, why shouldn't larger society represent the same family structure that resulted from different gender behavior?

Removing the glass ceiling

Today, the popular claim aimed to support a shared role for women in society is seen in such phrases as, "There are certainly biological differences between men and women, but none that should ever bar women from roles men have held." Is it conceivable that the positions men occupy or have held are really better filled by men and that different positions, no higher nor lower on a professional or leadership scale, would be more appropriate for women? Have the roles favoring the female been created in a society in which the phrase, equal for all, is prominent?

The positions we think about today were developed, not based on society's basic needs, but through the perception of the male to institute a measure of dominating, or more politely, managing control within society. This was made clear at the beginning of the twentieth century by sociologist, Thorstein Veblen.137 He claimed vested interests of men created the conditions of society which assured mastery over women. Although one might explain how qualities of the individual genders differ, that does not suggest that either gender could perform functions better suited to the other gender. How these functions are defined in support of society is more the question.

Consider the role and power in a classic example of male domination within a democracy: the president, not as the role has been portrayed in the evolving nature of democracy, but in how a democracy could behave more as a family unit than a geopolitical one. Should we think of a woman's "arrival" as her being able to serve in an executive role? Or, is there a different role based on societal need which would be more able to take advantage of specific qualities unique to women? What could such role be? Should determining that role be left to men based on their performance, or could it be more appropriately defined in terms of needs for democracy?

A simple truth

While it cannot be claimed that the Framers had any idea that women deserved a leadership role in the government they laid out, they cannot be blamed for ignoring elements of democracy in how government was to serve the interests of all citizens. Article 2 of the Constitution does not go into ap-

---

137 Veblen, Thorstein, The Theory of the Leisure Class, Oxford World's Classics, 2009.

preciable depth in explaining how the functions should be performed. It does address what functions should be performed, and that without much detail. Were it not for a long history of maleness appearing in the nature of the Executive would there be any prohibition against adjusting the means for executive leadership to accommodate the natural skills of the female? Could there not be consideration for executive caring rather than executive control? Does caring result only from control?

The Public Sphere has not been actively pursuing difference between male and female behavior as relevant in government. It seems only to consider the issue of compensation, or level attained by the female in order to justify increased compensation. Significantly, the qualities of democracy are not discussed in terms suitable for considering difference between male and female behavior. This discussion might have great value in improving the performance of government in a democracy.

Dialogue 28. Homosexual Marriage

The question of whether of not homosexual individuals should be allowed to marry can be discussed along two dimensions. Do two (or more) people who claim love for each other deserve to live together in marriage? Should either civil or religious marriage be the institution that binds them?

In either case, marriage itself requires a form of social acceptance in a democracy. Although several definitions for marriage appear across a wide spectrum of interest in any society, the one with less personal baggage appears to suggest a close or intimate association or union in which the participants live together in a mutually dependent relationship.

"Love is a simple thing; Love just is. That's all."138 Claims of love drive marriage relationships in Western societies, although other justifications for marriage exist. How long does love last? Is it, or should it be, for "eternity?" People who claim to love each other should be free to share with each other the expression of that love. We can make this claim if we believe in freedom for the individual. To the extent expressions of love are limited to the relationship between individuals involved, there is no social dimension to it. It is limited to the individuals who share it.

Marriage is claimed by the Catholic tradition as an outward sign of the union of love between two people. The State grants the rights, and limitations, of marriage. Why is involvement of the State necessary to grant and hold firm a commitment of love between individuals? What rights are retained by the State that gives it such jurisdiction? Is it part of the Social Contract? Should marriage be a social issue and thus under the aegis of gov-

---

138 Lyrics from a song written by June Carroll, first released in 1952.

ernment rather than only an interpersonal one? Is need for protection involved that requires the State to take action to support it, other than through any laws applicable to citizens, in general? Is there to be assurance of benefits? Is there more than a magical feeling that occurs for a couple in love when the State awards them a legal license?

The list of social benefits granted to a couple through the act of civil marriage is extensive, but some stand out in demanding attention. The way many societies are constructed today, a couple choosing to live together without the protective assurance of marriage suffers social stigma. In most cases, individuals living together, as married or not, benefit from shared family obligations. One of the individuals may be dedicated to maintaining a household, including care of children who might come into a relationship through other than sexual cohabitation. The other may provide financial means to cover costs of living. When one partner dies, burden for family-related costs falls in the other to assume the responsibilities no longer accommodated jointly. The State even provides a form of relief from taxation and other financial liabilities incurred when one partner temporarily can not perform duties. The latter is often cited as unreasonable when questions of marriage are not answered socially.

Social Stigma

Social stigma results from beliefs of society that same sex coupling violates cultural norms, limitations based largely on religious belief. Inasmuch as the government in place to vouchsafe the protection of citizen claims to set religious beliefs aside through an "establishment clause," such attitude representing religious belief might remain better at the social level and not enter the domain of civil licensing of interpersonal relations. If society believes such relationship to be inappropriate, why does its government have to be involved? It could remain more appropriately as an element of social culture falling outside the jurisdiction of governmental concern.

Either society accepts or rejects homosexual union as part of its behavioral norm. Homosexual couples would do well to seek acceptance outside societies rejecting their relationship. But why would society which believes in individual freedoms reject individual expressions of love, regardless of gender (or perhaps because of it)? There must be something else that rattles the sensitivity of the large segment of any population rejecting homosexual unions.

Religious beliefs

Either religion is a personal relationship between an individual and that individual's belief in existence of God, or religion is accepted by an entire society of common behavioral beliefs. In the latter case, a constitution is formed to explain limitations and allowances of power within smaller religious groups but subordinate to the larger social group. Sovereignty of any regulatory body is limited to serving the interests of that specific social group and its common beliefs, with no sovereignty applicable to a larger group. Simply, governance for any subgroup should have no sovereign effect over the government for the entire State. We should not have to be reminded of the "Establishment Clause" in the U.S. Constitution which rejects any relationship, sovereign or otherwise, between the central government and religious belief of individuals or of smaller societies of common religious belief.

Childbearing

In a religious context, the most troubling aspect of the issue of homosexual marriage involves children. Since homosexual couples cannot by their own behavior generate off-spring, at least at the time of this writing, we consider the process of adopting children from other relationships. Although the potential exists for one of the two individuals in a homosexual relationship to participate in creating a child, raising the child remains within the context of homosexual parenting.

It is not a matter of civil law that children are born. They come about through an entirely different set of principles found in nature. Civil law may determine who should be parents, but not in the process for how children may result from a physical union between male and female partners. If a homosexual couple were capable of generating off-spring, there would be no value in this discussion; it should be set aside as an element for science to address. Involvement of science to clone humans also is set aside for convenience, but not necessarily as irrelevant.

Civil benefits

In considering traditional marriage for heterosexual couples we note benefits associated with the elements listed above. Since the discussion of marriage for homosexual couples is joined in discussing civil benefits with marriage of heterosexual couples in a society claiming equality, why not grant them similar benefits? Society may claim that all benefits are not pertinent; perhaps they could be justified in such belief. Disqualification from any civil benefit would be a matter of law, a condition determined through representation of citizen majority choice.

Belief systems generally are driven by moral imperative. In a liberal democracy, oral imperatives for development of a state constitution are determined by laws of nature. Individuals also reflect laws of nature in their respective moralities. Individual morality does not reflect constitutional morality other than through a Social Contract.

Definitions for state benefits must accommodate needs of the individual when the individual reflects majority needs. Thus, if civil benefits result from the commonly accepted morality of the State's constitution, these benefits could be awarded according to how the State determines its obligations through law. No civil ruling should be necessary in addressing individual morals reflecting natural law, but if a majority accepts a need for benefit, laws could accommodate the need.

What is considered normal results from what has existed as accepted behavior by society. Time is the determinant for what is or isn't accepted. Civil definitions are neither necessary nor appropriate in determining what is normal by individuals regarding interpersonal relationships.

The issue for determining recipients of civil benefits, those created under law, is that the weak should be supported when they are no longer able to continue in their social capacity. In a liberal society, this supportive element is fundamentally important. Two reasons apply. One is that nature puts one of the individuals in a position of dependence, and society seeks to protect that individual. The second is that some individuals are born into an environment less supportive of personal growth and development. Liberal society decides, through civil law, to provide a shield of protection for these individuals. If a change is required to assure fairness in civil protections for those in need, it should occur outside the issue of homosexual marriage. It applies indiscriminately to those married as well as to those not married.

In the modern period, entering a marriage union is a matter of personal choice. Why should the tax code benefit couples in a civil sanctioned relationship over couples without such civil sanction? The only justifiable case is when the relationship disadvantages financially one of the individuals in the relationship, such as for the child-bearer or child-care provider. If the disadvantage comes from nature, as for child-bearing, liberal society may appropriately provide a measure of financial support. The idea in civil assurance of financial stability is to encourage population growth. This would have no relevance for any relationship that through intent or circumstance has little or no potential for creating of caring for children.

Insurance benefits

When one of the individuals in a relationship is unable circumstantially to earn a living, that person is disadvantaged from lack of means to purchase life or health insurance of any kind. Should there be accommodation for any relationship between couples to award insurance to one if only the other earns it? Perhaps it could be argued that insurance rates should be determined not on the income capacity of one, but the income capacity on the couple. In a case of a parent without income capacity there would be no change in accommodation. If both partners in a relationship earn income, there is no justifiable reason why insurance rates should be determined by salary of only one of the individuals, or on that partner's earning capacity (although the latter point might be difficult to measure). Society benefits from marriages, and civil accommodation through insurance should exist as long as societal needs are supported.

Two individuals might seek a relationship specifically to gain social benefits rather than to pursue a personal value specific to the relationship. No doubt we find some of both. The former should be set aside as an act of opportunism and not germane to this discussion which is based on what is claimed as a love relationship.

Do we need to review the incidence of divorce? How many children grow up in an environment in which one of the two natural parents leaves the marriage? How many children grow up in an environment thick in resentment between two natural parents living together, or when there is no natural expression of love between the two natural parents?

If marriage is intended to support child-bearing, should marriage survive the period of possible bearing of children, by intent? Should marriage as a civil union end when the intent (or ability) to create children no longer exists? Or, does the relationship survive on its own with a basis of mutual acceptance, even desire? Would the matter of choice beyond childbearing be different in a homosexual relationship?

Objections to children living under the care of a homosexual couple claim the child does not see the "normal relationship" involving only a male and female couple. Normal refers to something typically expected as a state or condition. Expectations in a democratic society are determined by law and influence what might be considered normal.

Other objections claim that children living under the care of a homosexual couple tend to become homosexual themselves. Here, we have a problem in definition. What is homosexuality? Does homosexuality pre-exist as a result of imbalance in natural hormone levels at conception, as example of one explanation, and thereby might be considered a "normal" for the medical condition? If so, civil law cannot change it, anymore than civil law or imposed practices change left-handedness.

Does homosexuality result from social deprivation? Should we expect civil law to assure each individual receives the necessary conditions to assure "normality?" Is homosexuality a matter of choice? Is civil law necessary to allow freedom of choice, or does such freedom already exist as a constitutional right? Is there empirical data demonstrating such cause and effect? Do data exist to demonstrate that homosexual behavior of children results at the same levels in heterosexual relationships?

Inasmuch as the issue of homosexuality is addressed in terms of legal acceptance, the claim against it fails due to lack of relevance. Along with it are the claims that homosexual relationships do not provide a stable domestic base for children and the religious claims that marriage is intended uniquely to support child-bearing.

A simple truth

While this discussion went astray of the title, it was to make a point that the issue of two individuals living together under civil protection is much broader than marriage. Considering marriage as the lynchpin misses the point of civil partnership. The following points are offered in summary.

- Two people who want to share living accommodations should have that right. Civil sanction should not be necessary.

- Individuals who choose to share living together do not need, nor should they expect, civil protection other than as granted among freedoms and liberty stated in the Constitution.

- Those who choose religious reasons to celebrate marriage should be entitled to do so.

- Those who choose to celebrate a religious marriage should not claim the right to impose their religious behavior on those who have different beliefs, religious or otherwise.

• Society should not grant benefits through marriage other than to address disadvantaged members of society, as accorded legally following the Constitution.

Child-bearing requires attention from society on other than issues of marriage. Adoption of children as a civil arrangement should be based on concern for care of the children and less on personal desires of those wishing to live in a family environment. Adoption laws should be based on care of children irrespective of rights for those choosing a parenting role.

Without diminishing respect for the personal feelings natural parents may have for their children, love from others can contribute comparable value to the welfare of children.

Marriage should not be a civil relationship; it exists as a natural element. But, civil protections should be available to individuals choosing to live together as consistent elements of social protection as existing under the Constitution.

Discussion of each of these issues should not depend on existing civil or religious restrictions or prohibitions. The elements are independent of social structure formed by law. They are elements addressed in openness of the Public Sphere. Law might result from commonly shared beliefs, but beliefs should not be restricted to existing civil limitations.

Dialogue 29. Immortality

According to the Catholic Encyclopedia, immortality refers to "... the doctrine that the human soul will survive death, continuing in the possession of an endless conscious existence."139 This seems an acceptable definition as it relates to transition between an existential state of human activity (mental as well as physical) to one we can only speculate about. The Catholic Encyclopedia continues with an association between what we can believe about spiritual things to what can be discovered from understanding science. "It belongs primarily to rational or metaphysical psychology ..., though it comes also into contact with other branches of philosophy and some of the natural sciences."140

Plato provides a different perspective for immortality. Although Plato accepts value in considering an after-life, he more purposefully explained immortality as a form, something that exists conceptually in the present as an idea, or eidos.141

Working from the here and now

Within the context of how immortality is considered from a religious perspective, some propose that an end will come to the human being as we know it in its present biological state. Hence, a fallacy is present in the no-

---

139 Included in a broader discussion of immortality found at, https://www.newadvent.org/cathen/07687a.htm

140 Ibid.

141 Plato's main argument for *immortality* is found in his Phaedo.

tion of spiritual immortality of a biological existence. Perhaps as Plato instructed, there is no after-life. Cybernetic science would seek to demonstrate how all important and necessary functions of the human exist in its current state. They can be transformed into a self-replicating entity totally dependent on automation technologies and devoid of weaknesses inherent in biological elements.

It might seem that a conflict exists in definitions of what constitutes living, perhaps in its present incarnation as well as in how living might occur with any transformation into a future state not yet known, or even knowable. The operative value is in the grammatical voice expressing living. We could accept either a passive form, characterizing a state of existence, or we could accept an active form, characterizing behavior.

A further element providing distinction is that in the behavioral characteristic we see influences not derived from predictability. That means, living is not deterministic, as might be characterized by a state of being. It is probabilistic, in searching means of survival and responding accordingly.

As we consider how life has transformed itself over the centuries of its knowable existence we learn through the sciences of examining both behavior and state of existence something similar to what we know as energy, causing life to continue even as it changes into different forms. Thus, we see the factor of evolution, or the transformation of the living element, to accommodate influences from environmental and inherent qualities carried in the species and transmitted genetically to off-spring.

From the conscious point at which the living can no longer continue in its state, or losing consciousness of it, we might ponder the likelihood that the energy that drives change in the biological form could be found influencing a subsequent host. Whether or not this has relevant religious meaning or not we continue to accept it without concern. But, if the future bodes termination or extinction of the biological form of living, how can we think of living in an active voice?

Would life in a non-biological form respond to programmed behavior? Programmed by what? we might ask. Is the programming also to be considered heuristic? Would such detection and reactive learning response to environmental need (for safety and continuity) be different from an energy seeking the same endpoint of survival?

Consider incorporating the notion of change in character based on environmental influences. If the automated form is not programmed to accommodate and adjust to environmental change, could it continue to exist in an environment of constant change? If a claim is that the environment does not really change, what value could remain for an entity responsible only for its continuously changing state of being?

Effects of near death perception

Scientific studies have shown that many people facing death claim to have experienced different states of being. They might actually reflect an event already experienced in their lives. Such state changing events might include heart attack, stroke, or physical trauma resulting from an accident. Some patients actually report experiences associated with an after-life event, such as seeing a bright light or an image of an already departed person or now dead favorite pet.142

Reported near death experiences carry a mix of both scientific and non-scientific explanation to assert existence of an after-life. But the issue of

---

142 A near-death experience research website to discuss such issues exists at https://www.n-derf.org/

immortality must be demonstrated by more than claimed evidence based on perception or on science. There seems no point in expecting immortality to consist of no more than what is already known or experienced. There must be at least new dimensions of thought, or new dimensions of awareness through other than intellectual comprehension.

A simple truth

It seems pointless to anticipate immortality. If subsequent or even previous life were to exist, it would be in relation to the experience each of us enjoys at the moment. Emphasis of value is on the here and now. What is demonstrated in the life we know either is inter-relational with an immortality or it is not. If not, there is nothing further to consider. If it does, and we might presume this to be so, our behavior should reflect what we are, essentially, or are in the process of becoming. Socrates tell us to "know thyself." One way to know oneself is through the eyes of others, found through discussion.

Dialogue 30. Education's value

Toward the end of the eighteenth century the developed world was beset with the idea of educating its populations. It had survived a series of wars, and life was settling down to reflect on the experiences. Universities appeared as vehicles for transmitting learning and knowledge. Developing dictionaries and encyclopedias was emphasized among the various approaches to education.

As the center of most systematic educational development, European states balanced interests in perpetuating societal values through two competing ideas for what sources of information should support educational demands of the public. One grew from the morality of the Church, and the other grew from a more intellectual challenge from existential awareness of reality through pure science or reasoned thinking.

Today, the debate on value of education is found in whether pure value from thought is more important than utility of education in preparing individuals for professional endeavors. The latter approach seems now to be preferred by larger educational institutions who compete for students and for corporate financial support. The moral basis at the heart of earlier thinking had been set aside for institutions specializing in moral training while general education considered it as impractical in a world emphasizing economic advantages.

Prevailing wisdom

Seemingly we all accept "wisdom" as an inherent byproduct of education. We may quibble about intrinsic or extrinsic value of wisdom. Some express their perspectives better than others express theirs. In the end, we bathe in agreement that education has value as it contributes to wisdom, the application of knowledge.

But do we agree on what this value is? What is the common purpose for humanity that it requires education in order to be fulfilled? Can we claim that an individual in our species is advanced in some aspect of humanity for having been educated after that individual exists no more? Is there a change in humanity by virtue of attaining a level of general or liberal education, of any kind?

Can we not feel a frustration with the notion passed from early Greek writers that one must "know thyself." We are told this, but following the application of at least Socrates it seems an implicit requirement of the human, along with the ability to apply it. One might expect to know (be educated) from an inherent need and satisfaction from knowing without having to be told.

Education provides the means to gain knowledge, to know. Presumably we experience as a revelation what we don't know from education. What source offers this education if not a individually-directed behavior to investigate essential elements of the self? Does self-directed behavior result from an energy discussed earlier? Perhaps we are left with a role for education in facilitating the process of learning, but how can we determine practical value from this application for developing wisdom?

Education for a purpose

Today's educational environment, at least in the United States, is business oriented. Other than for public education funded by the State, higher education is run in a profit seeking environment. It is highly susceptible to competitive power based on a complex arrangement of wealth distribution. Wealth is gained from those who contribute, profit from investment portfolios, from donations through private philanthropy, from government funds for public education, through enrollment costs specific to admission expenses and infrastructure costs. Education's expenses are balanced against expected financial gain from productive students and investors, and a few less tangible elements.

Where does this profile for education originate? Classical liberal thinking created a different starting point, but it had three different focuses, none of which can be found in contemporary educational institutions, not even in the locations where they originated. France provided its purpose in building institutions based on accumulated knowledge, featuring universities and dictionaries focusing on knowledge building, with the result of levels of social achievement. Italy emphasized value in moral teaching influenced by the Church from Medieval times and focusing on what was appropriate for education based on an ideal source legitimacy. Great Britain sought to expand education based on logic, explanation of value in application of knowledge.

As none of the earlier bastion of education remain as anchors for contemporary educational systems, could connection between classical Greek demands for knowledge be lost in favor of economic profitability in the modern world? Is education today no more than a facilitation of an existence in an impoverished state from lack of inherent moral value related to religious principle, from logic in application or from inherent accumulation of information for the mere sake of building knowledge?

A simple truth

Educational systems appear to exist at the pleasure of sources of capital to support them. Value for pure education, the thinking from the Enlightenment period, seems lost as capitalism requirements seek profit from investment. One suggestion to address the issue of educational needs, i.e., understanding, is to separate sources of education into two channels. One approaches value of education for its own sake. The second seeks value for what it contributes to the business economy. A suggestion offered is that the business environment cover costs of education as an investment. Education for its own sake might be covered by the State in seeking a well-informed populace.

What is the source of information supporting the Public Sphere? Collective knowledge supporting discourse might have different seeds for developing wisdom. But, the process of discussion ad debate should at least be supported, if not merely initiated.

Dialogue 31. Boko Haram

Reawakening of religious values occurred in the West through the movement of protestantism, a reconsideration throughout Europe of religious dogma based on moral principles. What began as conflict within the Holy Roman Empire between Protestant and Catholic advocates transformed itself across a thirty-year period to become largely one of different influences on governing for the nation-state.

The unresolved conflict continued long after the period of war ended, spreading through the United Kingdom and its colonies across the eighteenth century and found today in the United States in the form of protestant evangelism. The Christian community of the West (mostly United States) reflects a new purpose in spreading religious values inherent in protestantism as reawakening continues. Today, awakening is being observed differently as other than Christian moral values demand attention throughout the world.

Behind the mask of religious principle today one can find influences from Immanuel Kant as law, duty, and obligation anchor the practice of morality. For Kant, the obligation toward duty arrises from internal values for appropriate behavior.

An alternative to individual acceptance of moral principle can be found in the degree to which moral beliefs are accepted by the society. David Hume proclaimed a necessity to view moral principle by how it applies to observable behavior, a more rational application of belief. It reflects societal values rather than those of the individual as basis for determining morality. From interests of these two moral philosophers one can see a conflict resulting from different perspectives of humanity derived from values of living.

Applications of difference to explain conflict

The two largest monotheistic religions in the world today are Islam and Christianity. Both respond to common historical beginning but differ in interpretation of meaning and relevance for humanity. Islam demands strict obedience and "submission" to God's will as documented in the Koran; Christianity teaches a spiritual bonding between the individual and God based on good works aimed toward forgiveness of sin, as discussed in the Bible. Each faith-based religion proposes proselytizing as an element in its claim as the only means for attaining "everlasting peace."

As the world is experiencing globalization, movement from economic demands have forced elements of both religions into conflict, not only for individual acceptance, but for the spreading of governing principles. For each faith, everlasting peace seems an imperative uniquely assigned to each individual. Like the Jewish religion, Islam believes its existence requires statehood. Democratic Christian society claims its statehood is separate from religious teaching. Nevertheless, elements unique to Christian influence can be found in States in which the religion is practiced.

One example of extreme imposition of one religious practice on another is found in the behavior of Boko Haram, a militant Islamic group found in some African States. The method of gaining support for this group under Islam and to enable its own political program is violence, anathema to beliefs of peace and practices of "infidels."

The capture of hundreds of school girls in an attempt to gain leverage against both religious belief and politics raised the ire of other communities, even within other Islamic communities worldwide.143 Those in the West share a sentiment that behaviors of Boko Haram are abhorrent.

No acceptable rationale is available to comprehend its deeds, nor can justification of their nature be found in any school of moral thinking in the West. Should such behavior be categorized as terrorism based on how the international community is building resistance against violence from non-state actors? We can see violence, of course. But, could it be that such violence is expressive of a different nature, different moral values? Is it less human, even if reprehensible, than bombing a subway or flying a plane into a skyscraper or setting churches ablaze in Southern U.S., purposely to leave a political message?

One view at the moment is that a very long time ago (circa 1648), the political community was delimited by physical boundaries denoting sovereignty of States. It was a convenient if arbitrary determination for how social order was thought to be best implemented for the sake of peace (between the Church and monarchic leaders). For centuries following, people of the world community accepted this construct even if it violated social order for cultural communities not denoted by State lines. Any show of resistance to State sovereignty drew military response.

A few decades ago a precipitous event occurred demonstrating resistance from non-state entities against a social order which had different social values, ones not fitting nicely in the order of geopolitical States. Caliphates were not new, and remained in the fabric of closed societies with controlling ideals of statehood. Their manner of expressing dissidence was violence,

---

143 Discussion of the kidnapping of school girls in Chibok, Nigeria is found at, https://www.nationalgeographic.com/magazine/2020/03/six-years-ago-boko-haram-kidnapped-276-schoolgirls-where-are-they-now/

much as was seen in military warfare, and partially explaining the behavior of the Islamist Boko Haram.

The same motive was political for the sake of perpetuating religious values found in the larger hegemonic community. With Boko Haram we may be seeing signs of an additional transition for expression of conflicting social order, even if it reflects the sociology of the individual leader, behaving as a non-state entity on behalf of the community he claims to represent. Capturing females to assist in building population support was not the first time in history such behavior was manifest.

The world is not really a different place than it was at the time of the Westphalia treaties when sectarian solutions replaced vaguely located religious empires with city-states. However, rather than accommodating different religious claims through imposed geopolitical boundaries to separate them, order for common religious belief was claimed by attempting to develop sovereign rule by informally ex lege allowing influence by religious practices.

Today's conflict resolution is just experiencing violence in more forms than it can accommodate through bonding in attempts to gain order. It nevertheless compromises the potential power bases of sectarian government. If we believe, as some writers claim, that military power is largely ineffective against terrorism, and that police power is more appropriate, what could we now substitute for ineffective police power in the case of Nigeria, or Mali, or Cameroons?

Ultimately, should we expect the individual to provide self protection for him/herself? What role does that leave for police protection or military protection? Clearly, there is a role for each. Have we relinquished so much of our responsibility for individual safety and security that we can no longer deal with elements of violence through representative agents?

A simple truth

At the heart of religious principle lies the perspective of the individual. Whatever religious principle this invokes, a personal relationship with God is claimed. Legitimacy for such principle appears to depend on social acceptance, and then on the supportive government society. Rather than attempting to control violent behavior in the name of religion, could more effective results occur by educating the individual on his/her own personal values and needs? What form should this education take? Is there no value in social discourse, based on both education and experience? Must human society depend on faith to justify its perspective for humanity?

Dialogue 32. Phoenix took flight in Baltimore

It has been said that DNA cells of the fetal son pass from the protective shield of the mother's brain where they remain with unusual influence for the connection through life between the two individuals. With such physical connection is it any wonder that mothers and sons possess a close relationship?

Consider especially the story of Oedipus and Jocasta. The Oracle of Apollo at Delphi prophesied that the son born to Jocasta from Laius, the father, was destined to murder the father and to marry Jocasta, his mother. Even as Oedipus had been estranged from his family, the prophesy took hold.

Where does one find cause of something with a beginning far removed temporally from conception? Whether conscious or not, a strong influence of the mother on the son continues throughout the life of the son.

A display in public

What does it mean for a mom to slap her son around publicly for social misbehavior? How should disciplinary action be viewed, interpreted? As a teaching moment, it could be very advantageous for the mom to react immediately to a son's public misbehavior, assuming mom's reaction to be more constructive than harmful.

From recent history, an episode somewhat fantastic provides an opportunity to examine relevance of a mother-son connection. Many would not have an awareness of the event other than as a too often publicized expression of racial unrest, but the rioting situation in this case occurred in the city of Baltimore during the 2015 time period. The scene unveiled the fantastic regenerating flight of the Phoenix, arising from the ashes of its previous existence in social unrest to reveal a nature not well regarded beneath its public display.

We know it by observing it. We don't know from whence it comes, but it doesn't arrive without presence of a special human element that serves to provide some meaning for its existence. Here is a set of questions arising from the presence of this mythical bird.

A Baltimore mother slaps her son around in public because he behaves contrary to what she expects of him, and maybe expects of others. The son cowers and retreats. The video image of the event goes viral on social networks. The mother is congratulated for the discipline she metes.

Why does the boy cower? A bond exists between mother and son, resulting from something prior, maybe either conscious or unconscious interaction. One can expect that a measurable level of respect can be found on the part of the son for his mother and of the mother for her son. An observer might claim this event as tough love. But, what is it, really?

We can't say that a bonding love does not contribute to a resolution of this public expression of discipline, but the issue might appropriately be seen as a definition of what constitutes love. We don't see the love; we see the expression of it. But, that's not all there is to see.

For someone resident in the city, or with some historical residential experience, a jingoistic attachment could be expected. Perhaps an affinity could arise with the city to understand existence of a controlled tension between several different communities, each isolated from the other in a geopolitical cultural way. Each community is marginalized.

For Baltimore it was a smaller Philadelphia, similar due to cultural enclaves found in different regions of the city: Little Italy; Pollack Ville, Jewish Quarter, the Black Community, the Guilford Avenue nouveau riche, and poor white and lower middle classes nearly everywhere else. Each survives in a way unique to itself, and the lack of interaction prevents conflict, other than an occasional outbreak due to cultural overlaps, imposed by a corrupt political machine in order to maintain leverage against outbreaks, ironically. Everything is segregated, and boundaries are well known and respected. For want of a match, the city has always been on the edge of an incendiary explosion. Other large cities experience similar demography, and exist as potential for the occurrence of social, which is to say racial, unrest.

Without understanding any other significance for this demography demonstrated by a son caught up in a riot mentality and a mother responding instinctively to a relationship of maternal love, it can at least be observed to gain a sense of not interfering. Otherwise, we could lose objectivity by responding with the idea of establishing social stability.

What was the connection between the misbehaving son as one of the rioters in Baltimore on this occasion and his mother that prevented him from fighting back against the corporal discipline? Could that have been the missing ingredient contradictory to bonding an individual has with his/her community rather than with a parent?

Could the community express the same kind of bonding as found between Oedipus and Jocasta that might deter an otherwise undisciplined individual from rebelling? Is it sanguine connection that is missing between strangers? How can a community establish mutual respect with its members such that they could be "slapped around" from time to time because of unacceptable (if not illegal) behavior?

The female Black mayor of Baltimore at the time, much in the news, expressed her perspective as leader in such difficult times. She claimed it as an ability to compromise, a method to listen to both sides, she claimed, and to accept a middle ground of value such that ease of negotiating difference could be found. Madame la Mayor was wrong. Leadership requires more than compromise. It involves the mysterious connection that supports slapping miscreants around from time to time. Depending on the existence of community respect by the individual for leadership requires more than civil behavioral alignment to avoid revolt.

Hegel claimed that inherent in any existence is contrasting and polar opposites that operate for the sake of balance while the entity matures. Without the "negatives" there can be no purposeful value for the "positives." When the balancing occurs, if it does, we can visualize the reborn Phoenix taking wing. The rebounding bird provides no succor to the grieving. It does, however, allow the observer to see how dimensions for balance can be measured, understood, and contributing to rebirth.

A simple truth

What is fantastic isn't really beyond the dimension of understanding, so long as we are aware of its existence when it appears as a Phoenix arising from its ashes.

It is doubtful anyone would take the Baltimore event seriously enough to understand the fantastic element present, beyond its contemporary evidence of racial unrest. The socially polarized elements will see either how discipline is necessary, or that social services are abysmal, or that the police are by class abusive against certain communities, or maybe that something special exists between individuals to bind them. Generally, observers will insist on their respective biased positions with pointing fingers, and a social revolution will continue to evolve. Revolution doesn't have to be oriented to social positions. Personal interactions could be more effective in resolving social tension.

We see these things by identifying and discussing them. Value comes from interaction. It is not the sole opinion that dictates meaning, as meaning arrives from social participation which brings together different perspectives in reflecting the larger humanity involved.

Dialogue 33. Imposition of Nature's balance

Amidst several supporters and detractors an interesting debate exists regarding a tendency that all life, at least on this planet where the only life has been found so far, either exists in balance, as Herodotus claimed, or seeks it. The balance, or homeostasis, may be theoretical, but sufficient evidence can be found to suggest that the tendency may be real even though in practice it does not exist.

One way to think of balance is to remove all difference. As bland as this concept may seem it does help us view nothingness, the result of balance. For those interested in astrological explanations, balance is found in the Libra, the only sign in the Zodiac not related to a form of life. Thus, considering that no life is associated with Libra's influence we avoid the uncertainty of animal, which is to suggest human, behavior.

Anticipate balance as appropriate to nature

With every changing year, one poses that the past year was difficult in expecting the next year could be different, a little better. What may be envisioned is that the next year may become more normal to what is expected. The issue expressed by most if not all, for each of recent years is that there should be peace to replace world-wide violence against humanity.

Or, is the media playing tricks on us? Does balance really exist among all the perceived chaos but only as viewed holistically. Media takes the short view reflecting conflict from imbalance, a political perspective of those who sponsor news reporting. The result of this short view is that viewers note or anticipate transitions that represent normalization in action, one event at a time.

What we all have acknowledged at some time in our educated lives is that nature seeks a balance, that whatever forces are at work in one direction are by nature countered by opposition. Bodies of water seek a level; evaporated water falls in rain; winds blow to reflect difference in atmospheric pressure.

For many years, decades, centuries, many elements experienced in living have been believed undesirable, if not unsatisfactory. Humans tend to want to improve undesired conditions in order to make life, shall we say, peaceful and more convenient, resolving ill and travail. In doing so, circumstances are stacked precariously on one side of a natural fulcrum for which balance would otherwise occur.

Two dimensions of living show the individual and societal aspects of life, respectively. In an individual's existence control is sought to accommodate improved conditions of living - for the sake of comfort and convenience. In the larger society, accommodation is not so easy, as multiple perspectives for improvement contrast or contradict to influence compromise or other accommodation for difference. One person's gain is another person's loss. In the societal dimension the issue of balance-seeking is more pronounced. Natural conflict is resolved for the sake of balance if in unanticipated ways.

Even for the individual aspect, one may find strength in building accommodation against undesired elements of personal living only to have time disturb intent. What is built for the sake of comfort as often as not comes crashing down unexpectedly.

If one year is hoped to be better than the previous year, what might be expected to qualify as better? Is safety or security an objective? Safe from what; secure from what? Are these conditions of peace? Or, are they conditions of protection against life's tendency toward balance through change, even if unsettling?

Perhaps what is hoped for is merely an environment in which each individual, for himself or for herself and not for the whole society, can mask out inconvenience, or discomfort, to build fences or walls to ward off elements of life otherwise seeking balance. How long could such structure endure against unexpected collapse, or unanticipated destruction. A wall stops movement in both directions. In or out, up or down, the direction of nature is on its own to cancel out the differences.

"The wall collapse?! - not in my lifetime." But then, in whose lifetime? Does the individual outlast in time society of which it is a member?

For those who feel secure under current conditions, remain where you are and focus hope on remaining secluded, safe from the larger society, or from nature, or from change. Otherwise, be prepared for how life may apply balancing, and do think of tomorrow's tomorrow.

Is there a single element of living that could prepare or cushion against undesired shifting for balance? On the part of nature? Does universal love come to mind? A reasonable anticipation for any New Year and even for beyond is that difference will occur.

Difference is not to be abhorred. It serves to demonstrate the opposing elements in life which move in seeking balance. Positions far from the fulcrum only increase the pain and inconvenience when nature plays its role. Brotherhood may erase social advantage of one over another, as it could also ease us toward balance.

Construction of barrier walls

A contemporary problem for our age is the notion that immigration should be controlled, if not totally prevented. Uncertainty in immigration policy is examined by several groups, inside and outside governments. Since early in modern history walls have been constructed to prevent a balancing of populations between those intent on preserving a status quo and those seeking social benefits not otherwise available. Walls are a means of preventing nature from establishing an equilibrium between those who have and those who do not.

One notable element sought by emigrants is liberty, or the ability to chose for oneself what preferences would satisfy respective wants and needs. Opportunity elsewhere could promise such balance between need and satisfaction. A wall, by its nature, prevents attaining such satisfaction.

A trip through history provides an overview of attempts by one geopolitical entity that possesses means of satisfaction to prevent access by undesired encroachment. The Great Wall of China was conceived several centuries before common time, but continued its creation well into subsequent periods. The purpose was to protect against invaders, mostly Mongols, but even between different waring Chinese tribes. Approximately 100 AD, the Roman Empire created walls (Hadrian's and Antonine's) for protection against or to deter barbarians who marauded and pillaged from the north.

During the period following World War II, walls again were subject of political debate as East Berlin was separated from West Berlin by a wall to prevent citizen movement from East to West. Israel constructed the West Bank Barrier to prevent Palestinians from crossing into Israeli-dominated territory. More recently, the United States through the initiative of President Trump seeks to expand a wall between that nation and Mexico in an effort to control if not stop immigration of those claimed a threat against U.S. society.

Effectiveness of walls has come under scrutiny, almost at the same pace as they appear. While engineering marvels are observed, walls over long distances for lack of proper patrolling have done little more than stem rate of movement. Nature finds a way of resolving difference.

Humans, and indeed all forms of life as we know it on Earth, have existed a very brief period considering the age of the planet. Over this period very little is known to change the process of balancing. What might one find of more value for humanity as a whole in reducing the effects of difference from imbalance between societies? Humans have only caused efforts of nature to find alternative paths to accomplish what its natural direction imposes.

A simple truth

As we note the immutability of change itself, we observe a need to accommodate it. The conservative notion that status quo must be supported is a destructive one, even if it protects those who invest in a future designed to combat change, and thereby disrupt nature's intent for balance. Differences can be discussed, not to develop right and wrong, but to seek understanding that could minimize contrast and effects of conflict.

Dialogue 34. Runaway progress

Progress implies a relationship between a condition before change and a condition after change in which movement along a positive scale can be measured. Change involves a process to make the form, the nature, the content, the future course, etc., of something different from what it is or from what it would be if left alone.144 In measuring progress one expects to follow a path of being informed of benefit from opportunities, or progress can result in experiencing reduced threat or increases in a capacity to deal with them.

Oftentimes the value from positive change is accompanied or offset by liabilities resulting from addressing change. Accepting this liability by dealing with it is often overlooked, or simply ignored for lack of interest in accommodating loss. It could also be the case that decreasing risk of threat from one direction increases threat from an element in a different direction.

Too frequently people don't acknowledge accountability causing loss resulting from actions taken. Technologies to improve processing of information can result in psychological issues such as distraction, narcissism, expectation of instant gratification, and even depression.145 When the loss is accompanied by progress of a different sort, the loss is either dismissed or hidden intentionally. Treatment of both loss and responsibility for causing it are too often absent in commercial media.

------

[144] Miriam-Webster

[145] Discussed at, https://medium.com/@Muhammad_Muneeb/effects-of-technology-on-humans-health-755e69f53545

Over time

For so many years, decades, even centuries, society has congratulated itself on its many developments of progress, mostly related to technological achievement. Who can find fault with the value of fire, the wheel, combustion engines, the laser, and the Internet? Yet, for all the value gained, or claimed to have been gained, where does society find itself?

For each technological development leading to what is proclaimed as progress, what cost has been silently borne by much of society? As anyone could consider by taking time to evaluate any success, there has been a cost leading to unintended loss. Who bears the responsibility for this loss? Accountability for growth is arguably the least considered element when economies benefit from faster growth, lower cost, or from more convenience and expediency. Technological development in particular falls in this category of inadequate accountability.

In democratic forms of government individuals are elected as peers to represent voter social and economic interests in terms of how progress in government action is viewed. How accountable do we hold these officials to the basis upon which they gained voter trust? One might also consider what value is gained by those elected having been given this power and how the elected individual gains personally from how this value is manipulated? What accountability should be expected?

Considering how difficult it could be to find qualified individuals, who would also be interested in accepting the responsibility inherent in elected office? Would we be impeding government developers or political leaders from their purposes through demanding accountability for their actions or decisions?

In an environment heavily into research and development who spends effort considering negative results from successes? If the international community awards a medal for achievement, is there a related responsibility for the community to assure such achievement does not result in lack of accommodation for any overlooked segment of society?

Maybe the issue of better civilization depends on a different matter of morality. World development doesn't need to concern itself with "the meek," or with those with measures of intelligence lower than two standard deviations below the statistical mean. As long as development of new ideas or new services continues, increased economies and benefits of convenience for humanity could be advanced appropriately. We could believe that benefits for humanity are through the survival of the higher segments of population distribution while the lower segments are allowed to fall out of the corpus of humanity.

Should we permit through accountability those measures of responsibility that apply brakes on progress for social programs? If not, why the concern for social equality? Why do we express concern for the oppressed: gender, social standing, aged, apartheid?

Indeed, we could be concerned for the benefit of any future we could imagine. Any period in history, no matter who tells the story, demonstrates how marginalized social elements rebel against systems impoverishing them. As a world community shouldn't we therefore spend at least as much energy holding progress accountable for its claims of betterment as we do in evaluating how we have improved civilization over unfavorable conditions of our ancestors?

Progress from social networks

One measure of progress is determined by how different advances in technology and social participation in use of that technology produce improvement in the human condition without significant negative results. Results available through the technology is critical to evaluating how information access through advancements applies to issues of humanity. In regard to specific technologies associated with the Internet one can see a difference between decisions or beliefs influenced by data, or in opinion driven by content, especially as it reflects change in social behavior.

Value in use of the Internet is widely acknowledged. Access to visual images, status updates, videos of time-sensitive stories and personal experiences are all fundamental elements of how social media serves interests of a growing network of users. Social media is now a melting pot of all types of use, serving business interests as well as accommodating personal interactions. The seemingly endless variety of access methods spread commercial interests based on use profiles captured from prior Internet user behaviors. Largely without awareness by participants the Internet produces expansion in both demand and appeal. The world community may be approaching a status of over-saturation of content challenging mental or cognitive capacities.

While positive value is found through social network expansion through the Internet, an intentional or accidental byproduct is seen through shaming of individuals. Regulating such content considered destructive has concerned society a long time. Control against exaggerated representation of human behavior appears now to be a requirement levied on service providers or on those sources which manage distribution of content. Issues of citizen welfare supported by information access fall under the Social

Contract obligation accepted by governments to characterize the citizen-government relationship.

Regulation faces another element of concern as ownership of Internet is challenged by governments seeking to account for user behavior and content, but also to address growing business outside the domain of commercial taxation. As government becomes increasingly responsible for regulating advertisement content for the betterment of safety, health and security, it also addresses means of control in order to measure the extents of need and value.

The time when governments allowed social media platforms to be self-regulated seems to be approaching an end. Some governments have concluded that self-regulation in the market no longer works and thus they work to introduce new legally-binding measures to make tech companies responsible for blocking or removing harmful content on their platforms.

A simple truth

Two problems seem apparent in how the Internet serves interests of government, industry, and society. One problem concerns the issue of free access to information. Is access to information really neutral such that regulation is not appropriate? A second occurs in use of Internet content. Data can become a source of dangerous bias such that information represented in content distorts how users see a more objective reality? Does reality exist merely through acceptance rather than verification of appropriateness of information content?

Opinion is easily shared, but not often discussed. A truth may be found to support expressions of belief, but not completely. Discussion can open holes in rationality, and better representations of truth can be found in the Public

Sphere when open dialog occurs. Dialog is necessary to understand the basis for what is believed and why it is important.

Dialogue 35. Love Lost

Love is basic and inherent, indelible for the benefit of all forms of life, but especially to humanity to the extent its existence is acknowledged and applied. Love is an element of nature that simply exists rather than merely as voluntary expression. It results from imbalance. So does hate. It is an energy whose potential is purposed as a binding element supporting two necessary and complementary conditions.

As an element of attraction it is referred to as body chemistry, and has as one endpoint procreation of the species. An arguably more profound purpose than for romantic love is to bind the individual with others for the sake of common and congruent likeness of that species, as if originating from a single Aristotelian source.

Aristotle discusses the balance of life when activities of love and strife are balanced in a motionless "sphere." Immanuel Kant emphasized a moral imperative for the individual, certainly including the element of love, If Kant was correct, a broader but more profound morality exists for all of society that links individuals within that society, and as extension, all societies with each other to form a single human entity. Teilhard de Chardin referred to this process as convergence.[146]

With apology to the many couples who claim their love for each another as having lasted throughout the period of their togetherness, and even to have strengthened, such love demonstrates more a microcosm of societal love - society of two - than the "body chemistry love" that invites physical bonding - inside or outside marriage. Such incidents are examples of how

---

[146] Discussed in, The Phenomenon of Man, Harper's Torchbooks, 1955.

love can work when the attractiveness is based more on sharing common values of need and interests than in satisfying values that attract as energies of societal convergence. To the extent need continues, the marriage continues.

Love in marriage is shown to be regenerative. It is not the body chemistry element leading to marriage that endures. Enduring love is the fundamental element present in society that enables the marriage to endure after the body chemistry love has run its natural course. In too many cases, claimed love resulting from attractions of chemistry does not reflect fundamental love. It is not long lasting. If it were to last it would have benefitted from transitioning from body chemistry attraction to an enduring bond based on the energy within love.

A claim of love lost indicates fundamental love having never existed. More powerful than conscious behavior, love in its energy form persists beyond human decisions. Existence of love can be masked but can not be destroyed. Considering the four loves described by C.S. Lewis,[147] each example reflects the same bonding expressed in different ways, or representing different manifestation of it. (Lewis, on the other hand, claims them to be separate, each addressing different relationship and supported by different energies.) The religious element characterized in the Four Loves incorporates the religious expression of a force holding life to its immutable and fundamental form. Love is the single element binding all of humanity, as it does for all forms of life.

---

[147] Lewis, C.S., The Four Loves, Harcourt Brace, 1960.

A drive with a goal

In romantic, physical love, partnership is a means to an end. The end goal can be achieved when love is transformed from its inherent energy to complement mutual attracting desires of the individuals involved. The physical need which aligns specific individuals is only temporarily satisfied, and perhaps only partially, if only momentarily by the individuals who choose it. Even with civil bonding, satisfaction of need may wane. Nevertheless, need is inherent, as love is an element substantiating the human being. Romantic, physical love limits a person to an endpoint that neither attains nor even understands the full value of love.

Brain prints of individuals experiencing ecstasy of love are rational signs of existence of human emotional reaction to the influence of an energy form, but such evidence does not explain in any way what the element of love is nor what its goal is. Intelligence can be applied to signs and behaviors that reflect love, but that's as far as anyone, other than poets, have gone to express why anyone loves.

How successful in life could an individual be who claims not to possess nor to feel love? Decisions of monogamy are intellectually derived. They address more the institution of marriage than the coupling in love. One might pose the question of need to a person claiming to be monogamist. The response is likely to express lacking of personal need, at least lacking awareness of need. If disinterest in love is claimed, care should be taken to understand which application of love: romantic or spiritual, is addressed.

A simple truth

Celebration of love finds a place in virtually all human behavior. We claim it on different occasions, and believe we see it in others. No question is raised as to its existence. What is experienced, however, is not always consistent with these claims. Something fades; we find the pathway to continuous love blocked by the most trivial of circumstances. Love seems not to have the priority it deserves in the way we interact with others. Looking past the physical limits as a first point could provide view for its real bonding potential.

How openly is love discussed? Does verbalizing provide justice for meaning? As an intellectual exercise, discussion may also be complicated when discussants sense the energy characterizing love. If objectivity in discussion by such individuals could be expected, are discussants capable of the task?

Dialogue 36. Social content or deep meaning

A contemporary method for searching for deep meaning suggests use of artificial intelligence. According to Noam Chomsky, "deep structure" provides a means of understanding meaning.148 Deep structure provides a focus for understanding information - what it states and what it means,

Through the use of deep learning algorithms to process large amounts of data it has been predicted that pushes for use of Artificial Intelligence over the next decade would result in better capturing human abilities. These include all the human senses: vision, hearing, language use and other sensory cognition. Wouldn't it be interesting to understand meaning for the many senses we experience?

Until the present time, artificial tools have been used for purposes of creating new products for marketing to potential consumers. Discovering tastes and interests of social media patrons has led to directed messaging tailored to show available products to satisfy personal interests. More current AI activities suggest that focus for use is directed toward behavioral elements such as driving a car or interpreting facial recognition through patterns of expression. AI could, with the proper monetary attention that focuses on product development and distribution, be used for other investigations more aligned with determining morality of human behavior in accordance with elements of which the human is characterized.

With only physical evidence or recorded data to work with, the deterministic application for studying behavior would seem to lack potential for un-

---

148 Chomsky, Noam, On Language, The New York Press, 1978 (Chapter 6).

derstanding human values. How might deep meaning for behavior, for example, be discovered through AI? Can algorithms do more than examine results of behavior? At least at the moment, AI for human behavior seems only to focus on analyzing content from social intersections across the Internet.

While behavior, or any interest leading to behavior, may be reflected by individuals who post experiences on social media, the content derives through intellectual processes, searching through rational social content. The deep meaning that explains behavior is not available through methods native to the brain. No matter how much behavior is distorted through mental methods for explanation, cause of behavior can not be destroyed. It can only be hidden by ignoring or denying its existence.

Many are troubled by the concept of deep structure to find meaning. Appropriate definitions are hard to come by, but most would expect its meaning to suggest something more profound than what is observable merely by examining signs or behaviors.

A child playing in a sandbox reveals certain behaviors. Some behaviors suggest likelihood of cause other than the process of play. Anger could be expressed, as one example. What is the cause of such expression of anger? What is the angry child expecting, subconsciously, to express or resolve. Are there AI tools to apply to the images of behavior to provide answers of these "deep meanings?" Can dilated pupils, tightened lips, reddening complexion be interpreted for such application?

Meaning in politics

Politics is a playground for applications of deep meaning. Why did the United States invade Iraq in 2003, for example, other than according to justifying information provided by media sources or even found in discussions on social networks? Why do civilized societies execute criminals while expounding on the value of life? Why is there an economic wealth gap in societies claiming equal treatment, if not opportunity? Where does the patron of social content find answers to these questions? Is artificial intelligence a reliable approach?

Deep meanings for these behaviors according to many individuals have no value. To them, only observable characteristics are valid. Awareness of nothing "deeper" than statements and behaviors are needed for those who do not accept value of deep meaning. The press has a hay day, and so does social media. Content abounds. Yet, the superficial nature found in such "knowing" prevails to provide support for future statements and behaviors, equally misleading.

What is lost through dismissal of the question as irrelevant is understanding the nature of the human being who engages in an unending quest to know itself. Yet, in relying on superficial content, or content superficially, the individual cannot even approach an answer, even if one were available through rational discovery. Those who accept that no answer is available, or that the question has no merit, are satisfied to continue their respective journeys into a clouded reality. What might be the deep meaning in such denial?

A simple truth

Building a path of stones to cross the river has meaning for those interested only in getting to the other side. The meaning of the river, or even the need to cross it, is put aside as irrelevant to those who do not see the larger scenario consisting of elements comprising the whole. How else can one know what may lie at the base of behavior than by stating what is observed and through discussing its relevance in a deeper context. Such context re-sults from interaction in the Public Sphere. In a non-judgmental atmosphere accepted by individuals seeking better understanding of issues, one might expect all manner of behavior and belief to be discussed. Other than rational AI would be put to the test. Depth of meaning is demanded.

After Thought

The thoughts and ideas represented in the three parts of this book are suggestions for continued discussion and debate. Passing of time provides impetus for change, both in opinion and in circumstance. Thus, truth continues its uncertain path through experience of knowledge sharing.

No scientific rigor was sought to express perspectives in the dialogs presented. The Public Sphere does not operate on the basis of objectivity available only through careful development of support for thought. Rather, the suggestion that individuals capable of expressing thoughts and opinions comprise the only element needed to uncover a reality society would recognize and to provide reaction within it.

The Socratic environment for debate, suggested as meaningful for exchanging beliefs and opinions, is not dissimilar from what is found in the environment of the Paris café. As suggested earlier in these dialogues by Plotinus and later by John Dewey, any thought deserves the benefit of experience once it is expressed. Ideas in this book are intended to motivate action, both to test validity for the expressed ideas and to examine relevance of these ideas through living. Plato's Problem, expressed in the Meno as middle ground between input and output can be addressed by action - the method for gaining experience and lending value to thought.

There is no finality for any position expressed in these pages. Ask anyone in the Public Sphere of a Paris Café.

# # #